IT'S YOUR WORLD

Student's Guide to
Education Abroad

sponsored by StudyAbroad.com

Reasons for Study Abroad •
Selecting the Program For You •
Before You Leave Home •
Living Abroad •
Reentry •
Resources •

CONTENTS

Reorder Information:

Reorder information for StudyAbroad.com's- IT'S YOUR WORLD - Student's Guide to Education Abroad, single copy pricing and bulk rate order pricing information can be obtained at:

http://www.studyabroad.com/handbook/orders.html

Single copies: $7.95 (US) each
100+ copies: $2.00 (US) each

Questions regarding reproduction of this content for any reason should be directed to the company:

Educational Directories Unlimited, Inc.
1450 Edgmont Ave., Suite #140
Chester, PA 19013 USA
Phone: 610/499-9200
Fax: 610/499-9205
E-mail: info@edudirectories.com

A Pennsylvania corporation since 1992, doing business since 1989.

Intellectual Property rights represented by White & Williams, Philadelphia, PA

PART I: WHY THINK ABOUT STUDYING ABROAD?

Study abroad can be an enriching and eye-opening adventure, where learning extends to the world beyond the classroom walls. There is no substitute for living and studying in a foreign country if you want to gain in-depth knowledge of another culture's customs, people, and language. In addition, you will find that living and studying or working in another country can develop important transnational competencies that can be of interest to future employers.

PERSONAL GROWTH

Students who return from a study abroad program often see it as an experience which matured them personally and intellectually. They praise being exposed to new ways of thinking and living, which encourages growth and independence. For many students, going abroad to study is the first time they have really been away from 'home,' from familiar surroundings of the USA, as well as from friends and family. This is seldom an easy experience, but it is universally praised as worthwhile, often even life-transforming. After immersing themselves in a new culture, mastering the challenges of learning in a new and different academic environment, and experiencing the many highs and lows of being a 'foreigner,' students typically return home with increased self-confidence and justifiable pride in what they have achieved.

NEW PERSPECTIVE ON WORLD AFFAIRS

Study abroad can broaden your intellectual horizons and deepen your knowledge and understanding of international, political, and economic issues. It is almost certain that you will return from your sojourn abroad with a more informed and accurate perspective on world affairs. You will also have first-hand knowledge of how another culture approaches the tasks and challenges of everyday life, a sense of how 'global' the international culture has become, and an appreciation of the importance of international cooperation.

You will probably also gain a broader understanding of, and appreciation for, the United States, its way of life, and its role in international affairs. Through your professors, the other students in your program, and people you meet, you'll learn how others view the United States and its world role. If you live in a country where English is not the native language, or is spoken only by some, you will learn the practical importance of learning another language and using it.

CAREER ENHANCEMENT

But study abroad does more than promote academic enrichment and personal growth. It also can enhance your employment prospects, especially in the fields of business, international affairs, and government service. Employers increasingly seek graduates who have studied abroad. They know that students who have successfully completed a study abroad program are likely to possess international knowledge and often second-language skills. Such students are also likely to have other transnational competencies that graduate and professional schools and employers value just as highly: cross-cultural communication skills, analytical skills, an understanding of and familiarity with local customs and cultural contexts, flexibility, resilience, and the ability to adapt to new circumstances and deal constructively with differences. *(See From Toward Transnational Competence IIE 1997)*

WHAT ARE YOUR REASONS? WHAT ARE YOUR GOALS?

After considering these potential benefits, you must still ask yourself why you, yourself, want to study abroad. Take some time to think about your reasons, for they will become your goals and your personal measures of success. Perhaps you want to learn a second language, or perfect one you already know. You might want to learn about another culture, diversify your studies, or prepare for graduate school. Maybe you want to travel and meet new people. Whatever your reasons are, write them down and share them with your professors, family, friends and, most importantly, with your study abroad advisor.

There are a host of valid reasons for wanting to experience foreign study. Whatever your reasons, they should be positive ones. Study abroad should not be seen as an escape route from problems at home or on campus. Adjusting to life and learning in a foreign environment will have its stressful moments, and the more you are able to focus on your goals, the more you're likely to benefit from the experience.

The next section, Selecting the Program for You, is a step-by-step guide that will help you choose the program that is right for you.

Top Twenty Country Home Pages Viewed on StudyAbroad.com	
Indicative of most popular study abroad destinations	
1. Spain	11. Japan
2. Italy	12. India
3. Australia	13. China
4. England	14. Costa Rica
5. Canada	15. New Zealand
6. France	16. Cuba
7. Germany	17. Madagascar
8. United States	18. Taiwan
9. Mexico	19. Netherlands
10. Ireland	20. Ghana

PART II: SELECTING THE RIGHT PROGRAM FOR YOU

Section one

INTRODUCTION

Choosing a study abroad program that is the "right fit" for you is the best way to achieve your personal and academic goals for study abroad, as well as assist you with your long-range career plans. Therefore, it is important to plan carefully. However, when selecting the program, you are likely to get the most from involved careful planning. Hundreds of opportunities exist, more than ever before. They differ in location, duration, curriculum, degrees of cultural immersion, language, cost, and many, many other ways. Because there is so much to consider, it's smart to begin planning a full year before you want to depart. In some cases colleges and universities expect you to declare your intent to study abroad a full year in advance.

Start by realistically assessing your academic and personal preparation and objectives:

- What do you want or need to study?
- Do you need to earn credit while abroad, or would a work abroad program not for credit be possible?
- Are you fluent enough in a foreign language to take classes in it, or will it be necessary for you to take some or all of your course work in English?
- How much time can you afford to spend abroad, in terms of academic time and economic resources?
- Where do you want to go? Why?
- How structured or open a program are you looking for?
- Do you want to live in a dorm with other Americans, stay with a local family, or have some other housing option?
- How much money can you spend on tuition and fees? On housing and food? On international transportation?
- Will you need to apply for financial aid? Is it available?

This section provides information that will help you answer these questions.

Getting the most from any study abroad program requires open-mindedness, flexibility, dedication, independence, and above all, a spirit of adventure. Some programs, however, require more of these characteristics than others. Also keep in mind your adventure quotient when considering programs. Challenge yourself, but be realistic.

YOUR STUDY ABROAD OFFICE

Find out if your campus has a study abroad office. (It probably does if it sends more than just a few students abroad to study.) Study abroad advisors are experienced guides, especially in knowing what your campus supports and encourages. They can assist you in exploring all reasonable alternatives and help you sharpen your objectives for a foreign study program. He or she will help determine whether the courses you are considering will mesh with your educational goals—and whether you will receive academic credit for them. If your school doesn't have a study abroad advisor, consult the office of the academic dean, the office of academic advising, or a faculty member who is knowledgeable about foreign study programs. As described below, access to study abroad resources via written materials and the Internet is easy.

FIELD OF STUDY

What do you want to study? The largest percentage of U.S. students abroad take some courses in their major, while others take a broader selection. The most prevalent course work available overseas is in social sciences and humanities areas, followed by business and management; third in popularity are foreign languages. But programs exist in nearly every subject, from art to zoology. There are courses in animation, classical studies, chemistry, development studies, historical preservation, literature, marine biology, mathematics, the performing arts, physics, social anthropology, TEFL/TESL (Teaching English as a Foreign (or Second) Language), and women's studies. You can learn or polish a foreign language, including Aramaic, French, Kannada, Russian, Spanish, Swahili, and Xhosa. And you can study the people and culture of another country or region.

Academic Year Abroad and Short Term Study Abroad, published by the Institute of International Education, are comprehensive reference directories to international study for U.S. students. Peterson's also publishes a large program guide and has a Website listing programs. The books are updated annually, and contain information on thousands of program offerings. Programs are indexed by field of study—as well as cost ranges, sponsoring institutions, consortia, and special options—making these directories easy to use. IIE also has a very useful Web directory, at www.IIEpassport.org. In addition, there are various other Websites, such as www.studyabroad.com, which list programs and have hyperlinks to program Web pages.

EXPLORE A NEW SUBJECT

You might like to take an opportunity to explore an entirely new subject. Some students go abroad to take courses that aren't available at their home campuses. Others want to pursue subjects that can offer a richer experience when they studied in another country — political issues of the Middle East, for example, or the marine biology of Jamaica. If you are considering this option, find out how it will affect your graduation plans. Will you be able to meet your graduation and major departmental requirements? Will you need to spend an additional semester or year on campus?

FOREIGN LANGUAGE COURSES

Many students take part in study abroad to learn a new language or to perfect their skills in a language that is their major or minor. Living in a foreign country can make learning the local language much easier, thanks to abundant opportunities to hear it and practice speaking it. In addition, you may want to study a language or a dialect that is rarely taught in the U.S.

If you are interested in foreign language study, make sure any programs you consider are taught at your level of proficiency. Check program facilities: Is there a language lab? Is it well-equipped? Will you have access to a multimedia center or library? Will the credits be accepted by the appropriate language department at your home university?

ACADEMIC CREDIT

It is as important to make sure you are able to earn the maximum academic credit for your program abroad as it is to decide what or where to study. With the ever-increasing cost of a college education, no one wants to discover upon return home that credit for a semester or academic year spent studying abroad will not be accepted. Even if the program is offered by your home university, having the credit accepted and counted toward graduation, is seldom automatic.

It is essential to get approval in advance—and in writing. This may be routinely done on your campus or you may need to take an active role in getting approval for your study abroad program. Most colleges and universities only accept credit from programs that they authorize in advance. In fact, if you're receiving financial aid of any kind, pre-approval is required.

Find out if your campus has a procedure (or a requirement) for arranging pre-approval of the academic work you intend to take abroad. A study abroad advisor is the best source of help in this process. If your school doesn't have one, check with your registrar , faculty advisor, dean or admissions officer. These are the questions to ask:

• What can I earn credit for?

This varies from institution to institution and obviously depends on the level and quality of your overseas courses. Once pre-approval is given, this should make it clear if your overseas course work counts toward your academic major, or minor; or toward curricular electives; or simply as general degree credit. Be sure to find out before you leave where your credits fit in your domestic requirements for graduation. Ask if your school requires that you take a minimum course load in order to qualify for credit — it usually does.

• What kind of documentation do I need to have a course approved?

If you plan to enroll in a program offered by your home university, the description in the course catalog will probably be all your advisor (or registrar or dean) needs to approve it. If, however, you are considering a program offered by another U.S. university, you may need more in order to earn "transfer credit"—credit transferred from another school to your home university. Your study abroad advisor may request all or some of the following before you are approved for participation:

- The number of contact hours of the program: hours spent in lectures, labs, field work, etc.
- The course format
- Course outline and reading list
- Information on the level of the course
- The academic credentials of the teaching faculty
- Method of course assessment (exams, essays, projects, etc.)
- The grading system (ABCDEF, numerical scale etc.) and the lowest passing grade
- After you return, you may be asked to furnish your course notes, exams, papers, etc., before credit is granted or a course is certified as meeting a particular graduation requirement.

• Who issues the transcript?

The U.S. university that sponsors the program? A foreign university? You and your advisor need to know this. The same information will be needed if you are considering a program sponsored by an agency or a foreign university.

• Is the program abroad offered by a U.S. accredited institution?

Is the institution accredited to offer academic degrees in its own country? Your home university may require either U.S. or foreign accreditation in order for credit to be accepted. Find out your university's policies BEFORE you apply to a program.

• How much credit can I earn?

This will depend on your school policies and those of the host institution. Mostly, a 'full load' of courses passed overseas translates into the same number of credits which could be earned at home during the same time period. But not always, so get this clear in advance. Also, find out what minimum grade you need to earn in order to receive credit from your home school — usually, a C or higher is required. If your college requires that you achieve a grade of C or above, you may not be able to take overseas courses on a pass/fail basis because in many systems the lowest passing grade is a D. Therefore, ask if your school will award credit for courses taken pass/fail.

Amount of credit will also depend on whether the study abroad program is on a quarter or semester basis. If your home school offers classes by semester, and the overseas program is on a quarter system, ask your advisor how transfer credit is calculated.

In addition, universities may (or may not) grant credit for independent study, internships and other experiential study, as well as dissertation credit for graduate students who do research abroad. If you are interested in these types of credit, discuss the possibilities and the requirements with your academic advisor and the registrar.

In sum, be sure you know how much credit will be awarded for all overseas study and whether there are any tuition fees that must be paid to your home institution in addition to the fees for the study abroad program.

GRADES

Foreign universities may give a number grade rather than a letter, or even give comments in place of a grade. In addition, grading in some overseas universities can be much stricter than in the U.S. Transferring of grades to an American system can be complicated. Therefore, some colleges show only the courses and the credits you take, without recording the grades on the transcript. In other cases, grades earned abroad are listed on the home transcript but not included in the grade point average (GPA). Be sure to ask whether your home institution figures grades earned abroad in your grade point average, as this might affect which courses you decided to take.

Note: Most graduate schools, medical schools, and law schools will ask to see the original transcript from your international program. These institutions may convert the grades from abroad and include them in your GPA, even if your home institution does not.

LANGUAGE REQUIREMENTS

An important factor when considering a study abroad program is its language of instruction: do you need to know the local language in order to begin (or complete) the program? If so, how well? In some programs, some courses are offered in the native language, and others in English. For a number of overseas study programs, a specified degree of fluency in the host language is required for entry. Others require that you be willing to study the local language, perhaps at the beginning level. This, of course, is not an issue in English-speaking countries, or with programs in other countries that teach courses for foreigners in English.

You can evaluate your language skills either by taking a language proficiency or placement exam or by taking an appropriate foreign language class. Sometimes testing is done on the home campus, and sometimes programs themselves will test applicants (or accepted students, after arrival, to judge the level of their placement). How well can you understand and communicate in a foreign language? It is wise to be completely realistic about your level of competency. Being able to carry on a simple conversation in another language is no guarantee that you can do academic work in it. On the other hand, opportunities to make quantum leaps forward in your language proficiency are one of the reasons for studying overseas. You might be amazed at how much you will learn once you are surrounded by a language other than English and have ample opportunities to speak, read, and write it.

Many study abroad programs sponsored by American colleges and universities are conducted in cooperation with a foreign university or offer special courses taught by foreign faculty. In such arrangements, courses are typically taught in the language of the host country language, and generally require a minimum of two years of college study or the equivalent in that language. Some American colleges and universities offer language immersion programs to prepare their students for this course work.

A second choice is to enroll directly in a foreign university, where courses are usually taught in the host country language — or in an institute set up to meet the needs of foreign and visiting (non-matriculated) students. In either instance, you will need to be sufficiently fluent in the local language in order to be able to comprehend lectures—including academic and technical terminology—and read scholarly books and other publications. Most foreign universities and institutes require U.S. students to take a language proficiency exam before admission. If your language skills need some brushing up, many foreign universities offer visiting students special courses in the language, and others on the native culture and history. Note: direct enrollment typically means more effort on your part to ensure your home college/university approval of credit and financial aid transfer.

A number of study abroad programs offer some classes in English and some in the local language. With these, you'll be able to understand and participate in classes while you polish your foreign language skills.

Consider a program that offers all course work in English, plus a foreign language class (which is typically taught in the language being studied). This is an option within many study abroad programs, including short-term overseas programs, often held in the summer or a winter interim. But review the course offerings carefully, as such programs typically offer only a limited selection of courses. Whatever your foreign language skills, you're likely to have a better understanding and appreciation of your host country if you make an effort to learn the local language. Learning a foreign language in a country in which it's spoken is an entirely different experience from learning it at home. Because you are surrounded by the language in everyday life, what you learn in the classroom can be practiced everywhere you go. Even if you acquire only "survival" language skills, the people you meet will appreciate your efforts. This is likely to open up even more opportunities to practice your proficiency.

Knowing a foreign language can be a passport to many different countries beyond the obvious. French, for instance, is spoken not only in France, but Morocco, some West African countries, the Caribbean, and the Canadian province of Quebec. Portuguese is the native tongue of Portugal, but also spoken as the primary language of gigantic Brazil. And Spanish, of course, is spoken in Spain and almost all of Central and South America, and in numerous countries around the world.

TIMING AND DURATION

When would overseas study be best for you? How much flexibility is there in your academic schedule? How long a sojourn can you afford with your economic resources, even with financial assistance? These are major considerations you need to think about before choosing a program. In the past, most undergraduates who went abroad typically did so during their junior year, for the entire year. The majority were foreign language majors, or studied in English-speaking countries. Today, many options exist for study abroad across the curriculum;

for participating in programs which vary in duration from a few weeks to a calendar year; and for studying abroad at almost any point during undergraduate degree studies (or after one has graduated). All of these options exist — at least in theory. In practice, your college or university may have rules and requirements which restrict your choices a little or a lot.

Timing

When is the best time to study abroad? That depends on you and your degree program.. Study and living abroad can give you new insight into your academic goals, so taking part in this experience early in your undergraduate education—typically at some point in the sophomore year—can help provide academic direction. If, however, you have strong academic interests that you would like to explore beyond the boundaries of your home campus, study abroad might be more appropriate in your junior or senior year. Be aware that some universities don't allow senior year study abroad, and some allow it only in the first semester of the year. Be sure to check with your campus study abroad office regarding institutional policies.

Duration

How much time do you want to spend studying abroad? Study abroad advisors, from long experience listening to returned students generally counsel that the longer the program and the more immersed in the local culture you are, the greater the long-range benefit.

Academic Year or Semester: About half of all U.S. students current studying abroad are participating in semester or academic year abroad programs. Such programs, because of their length and opportunities for true immersion in a foreign culture, are likely to make the strongest and most long-lasting impact both academically and in terms of cross-cultural understanding and career preparation. It takes time to adjust to a new living and learning environment, and many would say that the best learning takes place after such adjustment has taken place. But there are other issues to consider. Do you have the discipline to pursue your studies for a semester or year away from home? Can you afford to spend that much time away from your academic program? If the answer to either of these is "no," there are still plenty of study abroad options available to you. About half of all U.S. students now studying abroad do so on short-term programs; that is, programs shorter than an academic semester. Shorter programs, if well-planned, can offer a more intensive and focused experience— and may be the only realistic alternative in terms of the demands of your degree studies and economic resources.

Summer study programs range in length from two weeks to three months, with the largest number offered for one to two months. You can combine academic course work with program-related travel, or course work can be followed by vacation travel. Sometimes the program is entirely travel (in which case earning credit may not be possible). Such programs are sponsored both by American higher educational institutions, as well as by overseas universities, agencies, and organizations. So-called 'vacation' study programs are enormous in number and variety. Such programs are offered all over the world. You can study business law in Australia, fashion design in London, U.S.-Mexico relations in Mexico, and international finance in Tokyo. Programs range from two- or four-week courses to those that last two or three months. Courses of study vary from those with a strong focus on academics, with the addition of a few field trips, to a study tour, in which travel and learning are combined. Vacation and summer study programs are sponsored by U.S. colleges and universities and foreign higher educational institutions. Many specialized institutes abroad focus on the art, language, and culture of their home countries and offer short-term programs to U.S. nationals.

Interim study programs are held in the period between semesters, especially for universities on the 4-1-4 calendar, or between academic quarters for those operating on the quarter system.

Pre-freshman year programs are available for students who feel they need a breathing period between completing high school and beginning college.

Follow-up or Lab programs, led by the instructor, are held to supplement what was learned in class with first-hand, on-site, exposure to what was studied.

Some language study programs are sponsored by language-teaching institutes, e.g., Alliance Française, Goethe Institute.

Also available are 'study tour' programs in which a U.S. professor leads a traveling group of students, alums, or others within one country or to several countries, for credit or just the educational exposure.

LOCATION

Europe or Elsewhere Throughout the World?

Where is the best place for you to study? The answer obviously depends on many different personal, curricular, and institutional considerations. Think this through carefully, as no given place is likely to answer all your needs, and yet each place has something unique to offer. Western Europe is the traditional destination for American students going abroad, and now accounts for about two-thirds of all students. One of the reasons students head for Western European countries is because there are so many well-established program sites there. Yet programs now beckon from all over the globe.

But, in increasing numbers, students are also deciding to consider other regions, sometimes based on course work, sometimes on language, cultural, or career interests. Excellent programs are available in the former Soviet Union, Eastern Europe, the Middle East, Africa, Asia, Latin America, South America, the Caribbean and the islands of the South Pacific. In fact, almost (but not quite) everywhere! You can study volcanology in Costa Rica, political change in South Africa, Buddhism in Tibet, or indigenous music in Zambia. Nothing can compare with learning a foreign language in a country where it's spoken, whether that means learning Spanish in Spain or Wolof in Senegal.

Living and learning in a culture that is dramatically different from one's own can provide an incomparable learning experience, challenging customary assumptions about one's own society and values and providing a unique perspective on the larger world. The fact that nearly three-quarters of the world's population live in 'developing' nations is bound to have a significant effect on the course of history. From an economic standpoint, it is worth noting that U.S. trade with developing countries now approaches 40 percent of all U.S. imports and exports. In today's economically interdependent world, knowledge of developing nations may prove to be a tremendous career asset. One legacy of colonialism in these culturally diverse and economically emerging countries is that the language of instruction in higher education is often English, Spanish or French rather than the native language. This does not apply, however, to countries like China, which has an extensive scientific and technical literature of its own, and which draws large numbers of students to study its literature, languages and cultures.

In Search of Roots

Some students go abroad in search not of the new, but of what they hope and assume will accord with their own family background, whether ethnic, religious, or national. Students from Arabic-speaking families thus sometimes wish to study in the Middle East, Hispanic students might select any of the countries where Spanish is spoken, Jewish students might opt for Israel, African-American students might be interested in one of the many programs in Sub-Saharan Africa, and Asian-American students may look to programs in the Orient. If this is part of your motivation, you are likely to find rewarding connections to your background. But be prepared to find that, no matter how fluently you speak the local language or how closely you resemble the local people, you will first of all be treated as 'an American' by the local population.

Big City Vs. Small Town

Do you want to study in a big city? A small town? A rural area? A large city offers a wide array of social choices and many cultural opportunities, but it can also be expensive, impersonal, and more cosmopolitan than national in its identity. Aix-en-Provence is perhaps a more 'French' city than Paris, Tampere a more 'Finnish' city than Helsinki, for instance. On the other hand, a provincial town or rural area can offer a traditional way of life and more contact with local residents, but its narrower lifestyle may be too confining for some.

One place or many?

Do you want to spend most of your time in one place, or travel to several places? Would you like full-immersion in one culture or comparative glimpses of many, in pursuit of common themes or issues - e.g., environmental pollution, national health care systems, the treatment of minorities, etc.? While the majority of study abroad programs are based primarily in one location, with occasional excursions to other nearby cities, a few programs involve some or even considerable travel. A program of studying wildlife ecology in Kenya, for example, will probably include a number of excursions from the classroom to game reserves. Other programs use travel as a means of comparing and contrasting differences. One program on Ecuadorian ecology takes students from the capital city of Quito to a small village, through the Amazon rain forest, and to the Galapagos Islands. Another looks at issues affecting women in England, the Netherlands, and Germany. Yet another contrasts business management assumptions and policies in Korea, China, and Japan.

PART II: SELECTING THE RIGHT PROGRAM FOR YOU

Section two

ENROLLMENT OPTIONS

Approximately 72% of U.S. undergraduates who end up studying abroad enroll in a study abroad program specially organized for students like them. The sponsor may be a U.S. college or university (the student's own, another, or a consortium) with which it has reached an agreement. Or the sponsor could be a domestic organization other than a college or university, or an overseas university or organization, often as part of its program for other international students. However, depending on your own institution's policies with regard to transfer credit from other domestic or overseas institutions, a host of other options may exist for you. The below list moves from options centered in your own institution to options more centered in overseas institutions.

Enroll in a Program Designed and Overseen by U.S. Colleges or Universities for American Students

The most popular choices of study abroad programs include those sponsored by a student's own institution, by another U.S. college or university, or by a consortium, or group, of U.S. colleges or universities. Such arrangements make possible hundreds of academic year, semester, quarter, and vacation study program opportunities.

Programs sponsored by U.S. colleges allow students to study in a foreign environment while remaining within an U.S. academic framework. Even if the actual course work is taken at a foreign university, academic credit is arranged through the sponsoring U.S. institution. In many cases, special courses in the language and culture of the host country are offered, and the language requirements may be relaxed. The sponsoring college usually also makes housing and round-trip travel arrangements for students, and may arrange cultural excursions.

Programs offered by U.S. institutions basically fall into two main categories, though many variations exist within each:

- The "island" program: All courses are arranged for a group of U.S. students and taught by home campus faculty members familiar with the host culture or by foreign faculty hired by the U.S. school. Costs are often about the same as study on the home campus, and financial aid that you receive from your institution or from the government can typically be used. Some of these programs offer intensive language study for language majors. Generally, though, these programs are taught in English, except for foreign language classes, which are taught in the language studied. This is a good option for students who don't speak the local language. It may also be a good choice if this will be your first time overseas. Be aware, however, that no overseas program can provide academic and social services identical to what you are accustomed to at home.

- Hybrid Programs: Study in a foreign institution, combined with courses arranged for the group by the sponsoring U.S. institution: These programs generally require some knowledge of the host country language. Nonetheless, special university courses for U.S. or other foreign students usually have less demanding language requirements than regular university courses. And some programs offer a choice of foreign institutions, depending on the level of the student's language skills. One benefit of this type of program is that it lets you study at a foreign institution while meeting requirements for your U.S. degree. Many of these programs also offer academic support services similar to those found on a U.S. campus.

Enroll in A Program Sponsored by an Organization Other than a U.S. College or University

Some not-for-profit and for-profit organizations in the U.S. and overseas also sponsor study abroad programs. Of these, some have agreements with colleges and universities allowing students to be registered on their home campuses. Others indicate that academic credit is available or transferable, but students must arrange or verify the credit themselves. If you are considering one of these programs, be sure to investigate your school's credit transfer policy, as well as the policy of the program you are considering.

Enroll in a Program for International Students at a Foreign University

Some universities abroad offer language and culture programs to foreigners. These enable U.S. students (considered 'international students' while overseas) to interact with students from several other countries. Some programs sponsored by foreign universities are especially designed to meet the needs of English-speaking students, with courses offered in English as well as the host country language. In addition, in the 1990s, as academic mobility and exchange in Europe increased, a number of English-language programs were designed for students from other countries. Some of these are available to U.S. students as well.

If you want to enroll in this kind of program, be sure to discuss credit transfer with your advisor. In some cases, foreign schools arrange to transfer credit through an accredited U.S. college. But credit doesn't transfer automatically from foreign universities, and in some cases is not transferable.

Enroll in A Foreign University Via a U.S. College or University

It is also possible to enroll in foreign universities directly by applying through U.S. programs set-up for this purpose — e.g., Arcadia University's Center for Study Abroad or Butler University's Institute for Study Abroad. This intermediation can solve the credit transfer problem, as the overseas course work is placed on an American college transcript. Such a process can increase overall costs, but, in return, may also provide orientation, accommodations, excursions, and on-site support services not otherwise available to occasional or special students.

Enroll Directly in a Foreign University As a 'Special' Student

Many universities around the world are open to students from other countries who qualify for admission as 'special' or occasional students. This is similar to taking regular classes in the United States as a non-admitted or part-time student. Credit does not transfer automatically from foreign universities and in some cases is not transferable. Taking classes taught by foreign teachers, alongside students from the host country, can be very exciting and challenging. But it requires an extra measure of enterprise and resourcefulness on your part, since it's up to you to make the arrangements and do the course work without support services from an U.S.

institution. You also must be fluent in the language of instruction to consider this option. And there can be difficulty with credit transfer as well with the transferability of your U.S. financial assistance.

In many foreign countries, students can receive a secondary school education that is more advanced and intensive than what U.S. high school's or preparatory academies offer, with students graduating at the age of 19 or older, then sometimes waiting another year or so before beginning their university education. These students may have the same academic preparation as an American student who has completed two or more years of college. For this reason, even foreign universities that accept American undergraduates into degree programs may do so only after they have completed their sophomore year.

If you are interested in this option, addresses of most foreign institutions can be found in World of Learning or the International Handbook of Universities, reference directories on higher education worldwide that can be found in many U.S. college and university libraries. To ensure a response, enclose an International Reply coupon (available from any Post Office) with your inquiry. An easier way to find out whether you should even consider applying for admission to an overseas institution is to do a Web-search and pursue your interest through foreign university Web pages. Again, your study abroad advisor may also provide guidance.

OTHER STUDY ABROAD OPPORTUNITIES
There are yet additional options for acquiring overseas education. You can:

- Attend a branch campus of a U.S. college or international university abroad.
- Set up an Independent project to be carried out overseas. Some, but certainly not all, U.S. colleges and universities offer independent study arrangements in which qualified students carry out pre-approved research or in-depth study projects in a selected field or on a special topic. It is your responsibility to complete the study or conduct the research, typically evaluated by a faculty advisor when you return home.
- Pursue course work, language learning, research, or an internship overseas after graduation, with no expectation of credit, but increasing your credentials and career pursuits.

Housing Options
Your living situation will have a significant impact on your study abroad experience. Housing can be as grand as a manor house, as rugged as a tent in a rain forest, or as standard-issue as a university residence hall.

Many study abroad programs provide student housing. Some arrange home-stays, in which you live with a local family. Others provide housing in dormitories or apartments, where your roommates could be students from the host country, from other foreign countries, or from the United States. For short-term programs or those that require extensive travel, students may be housed in hotels, pensions, or student hostels.

Some programs offer a choice of housing arrangements. In most cases, however, the choices are few, as student housing is difficult to find almost everywhere. Dormitory space is often so limited that many foreign universities have strict quotas for the number of rooms allotted to international students.

Be sure to find out whether programs you are interested in arrange housing for participants; not all do. If it's up to you to find your own housing, ask if the sponsoring institution will assist you. Request an estimate of costs for accommodations, food, travel and essential living expenses.

Living in Dorms or Apartments

Most students live in dorms or apartments while studying abroad. Some single rooms may be available, but two or more students to a dorm or apartment are more common. Depending on the program you select, you may have a choice of the nationality of students you room with.

Living with other U.S. students:

Surrounded by experiences that are new, some U.S. students are most comfortable living with students from their own country. However, if cultural immersion, cross-cultural learning, and/or an intensive experience of the host culture are high on your list of goals, you may wish to live with students from the host country.

Living with students from the host country or other foreign countries:

You may opt for this if you consider your living situation to be part of your overseas learning experience. If you want to live with local students, be aware that, in some countries, local students live in dorms only for their first year, then move to apartments.

Many universities abroad put all foreign students—including those from the U.S.—in a special dorm for foreigners. While, you are unlikely to meet host country students in these dorms, you will be surrounded by other students sharing the experience of being new to a country.

Home-stays

Home-stays usually provide the greatest immersion in the host language and culture, giving you the opportunity to experience how local people really live. This is especially true if you live with a family that treats you like one of the family, getting to know you and offering help if you need it.

In some cases, however, the host is simply someone with an extra room to rent out, and your relationship is strictly that of landlord/tenant, with little or no social interaction.

In many cases, you will not know the name or address of your home-stay until you arrive at the program. This is a major difference between college-level study abroad programs and high school exchanges.

Smoking is far more common—and accepted—abroad than in the U.S. If a nonsmoking environment is important to you, find out if anyone smokes in home-stays you are considering, or ask for a nonsmoking roommate in dorms and apartments. But be prepared to learn to live in an environment where people smoke.

If you are a Vegetarian or Vegan, or if you have other special dietary needs, check to see if these can be accommodated. Vegetarian menus are not common outside of the United States, especially in Europe. If you are living with a host family, it may be perceived as rude for you to refuse the meals they serve.

In many cases, it may be a hardship for the family to provide separate meals for you. Please be clear about your needs before the program places you in a home-stay situation as it may not always be possible to accommodate your special requests. And be prepared to compromise with regard to your dietary choices. Remember, you are the guest. You may also have to bear the extra costs of special meals yourself.

Housing Specifics

Get as much information as possible about housing. This can help you decide whether a program is for you, or at least prepare you for what to expect.

For programs in any country, ask:
- What kind of furnishings does a dorm or apartment have?
- Is there a desk or table for you to work at?
- Is the kitchen equipped with cooking utensils?
- Does a dorm provide sheets, blankets, pillows etc.?
- If not, Is there a service available to rent linens?
- Are there laundry facilities?
- If so, are these automatic washers or laundry tubs?
- Is there a limit on how often you can use them?
- What is the cost?
- Will you have access to a phone in your residence?

If you're planning to study in a developing country, ask your program representative:
- Is there drinking water available?
- Is there hot water for showers?
- Is electricity always available?

Last, remember to confirm all housing arrangements well ahead of your departure.

HOW TO RESEARCH STUDY-ABROAD OPPORTUNITIES

Once you've considered fully what kind of program is right for you, you're ready to research what's available to fit your complex needs and interests, resources, and time. Most students begin by investigating those programs directly sponsored by their own campus. Some schools indeed limit their students to their own programs, providing information only about these programs (and, sometimes, affiliated programs) and erecting a host of academic and/or economic disincentives meant to discourage students from participating in programs sponsored by other institutions. Others have lists of programs pre-approved for transfer of credit, which may or may not qualify for institutional financial aid. Yet others have an open policy, allowing students to choose from the hundreds and hundreds of available programs which are open to any qualified student. If your school doesn't sponsor study abroad programs (or doesn't offer the 'right' program for you) or you want to look beyond your home campus course offerings, there is a wealth of information available today, from many different sources, on programs of all types.

Campus Advisors

If your school has a study abroad office, talk to a study abroad advisor about how and where to research programs. If your campus does not have a study abroad office, ask your academic advisor for help in researching your options. He or she may be knowledgeable about international study, or may be able to refer you to faculty members who are. You should also talk to your school registrar or someone in the admissions office about your school's policies on study abroad, especially if you are considering a program that is not sponsored by your school. Also, if you'd like credit in your major for study abroad, be sure to see an advisor in your major department.

Campus Study Abroad Library

Many U.S. colleges and universities have a study abroad library, or a section of the college library that is devoted to study abroad. A good study abroad library will have reference books containing thousands of listings of study abroad programs, as well as catalogs of study abroad programs from other U.S. institutions, and foreign university catalogs — the best reference guide is *Academic Year Abroad and Short Term Study Abroad,* published by the Institute of International Education. Ask an advisor if there are brochures for individual programs, or videos, slides, CD-Roms, or photos of programs and program sites. Your campus study abroad library may also carry the magazine Transitions Abroad, with articles about study, work, and travel abroad written by recently returned student participants (also see the magazine's website, *www.transitionsabroad.com).* In addition, many study abroad libraries have written evaluations of programs from recent participants. This kind of unbiased first-hand information usually cannot be found elsewhere.

Searching The Internet, the World Wide Web, and Education Databases

In recent years access to information of all sorts on international education, via new telecommunications technologies, has burgeoned. No longer are you limited to what your particular campus has on its library shelves or what you can write for to be sent to you. Volumes of valuable information on nearly every aspect of study abroad is now immediate from any personal computer or campus network. Using this technology to find Web-pages, you can gather information on hundreds of programs and foreign universities; on financial aid: scholarships, fellowships, and grants specifically geared to study abroad; on internships and volunteer opportunities; on international travel; on particular countries or specific fields; on getting your passport and visa requirements; on health and safety conditions; and on international currency exchange rates and banking. Information alone will not be sufficient, so it should be gathered, studied, and discussed with your campus advisors and fellow students. A few of the best sites to start with are:

www.IIEPassport.org, Institute of International Education; includes IIE's books *Academic Year Abroad and Short Term Study Abroad,* in database format, as well as scholarship information.

www.StudyAbroad.com, providing online directories of programs and destination information plus links to leading providers.

www.nafsa.org/secussa, (click on "Internet Resources") the site of NAFSA: Association of International Educators; has links to the best websites for study, work and travel abroad.

Talking With Returned Students

If you are interested in a particular program, talking to students who have recently taken part in it is often the best way to find out what it's really like. Be aware, however, that no two students on the same program ever have precisely the same experience or response, and you may have different goals and interests. You might ask: Did the course load leave time for socializing or traveling? Is an ability to get along with others essential on this program? Is the optional safari — or scuba diving expedition or trek to see ancient ruins — worth the extra time and money? And the like. Your campus may organize group sessions with these students, or give you contact information for them so you can talk to them individually.

If it's not possible to talk to students who've been on programs that interest you, talking to students who have taken part in any study abroad program will be useful, since you'll hear about what it's like to live and study in a foreign country. Many campuses use returned study abroad students as 'peer counselors.' If yours does, make sure you tap into their seasoned perspectives. Of course, it's best if you can find students who studied in the country or region you're considering. If you're considering studying abroad through a program not sponsored by your school, ask the program for telephone numbers or e-mail addresses of students who have attended that program. These may be carefully selected individuals. Still, be wary of a program that refuses to let you contact previous participants.

Talking with program representatives can provide invaluable insight and information which is direct and personalized. Many campuses arrange for occasional campus visits by such people. Some also set up annual Study Abroad Fairs, at which representatives from many different study abroad programs, as well as from organizations sponsoring internships and voluntary work programs, are present throughout a given day or evening, to talk with interested students. There may also be students present who have participated in particular programs. If such opportunities present themselves (on your own or a nearby campus), you should definitely take advantage of being able to collect current materials, ask questions, and gain insights from persons who know their program from direct experience.

Even the best reference book or catalog has only general information about programs, and brochures may focus more on the local attractions and nightlife than on academics. After you've identified programs that interest you, check the programs' websites, e-mail, call or write the sponsoring institutions for detailed information and application forms. And it's always best to call a program and speak with its advisors to discuss questions that remain unclear after you've read program booklets. Many programs, especially larger and more established ones, allow the 800 number or e-mail address to be used for the purpose of providing you with additional information, answering your and your parent's questions on a one-to-one basis — and, when you are ready, taking an application.

Top Ten Languages Searched on StudyAbroad.com	
Indicative of most popular languages studied abroad	
1. English	6. Italian
2. Spanish	7. Arabic
3. French	8. German
4. Japanese	9. Swedish
5. Chinese	10. Thai

PART II: SELECTING THE RIGHT PROGRAM FOR YOU

Section three

COSTS

In order to encourage students to study abroad, most U.S. institutions do their best to try to keep the expenses of overseas study comparable to the cost of the same period of study at the home campus. How much will studying abroad actually cost you (and your parents), especially in relation to what study at home costs? There is no simple answer to this major question, other than that participation in any given program can add up to somewhat less or much more, depending on a host of factors — some of which are controlled by your institution (e.g., its tuition policy, whether it sponsors its own programs, whether financial aid travels, etc.); some of which are matters over which American institutions may have no control (e.g., international currency exchange rates, overseas costs of living, university tuition costs, etc.). In short, the absolute, overall cost of an overseas study experience is something apart from how affordable it is to any given participant.

VARIABLES

Many U.S. sponsors of study abroad programs bundle the program's major costs into one comprehensive fee. This usually includes tuition, housing, meals, and international airfare, and may also include medical and accident insurance, excursions, books, rail passes, and other program-related expenses. Others may include some, but not necessarily all of these items. Since all are likely to be relevant to figuring out overall costs, it is your and your parents' responsibility to ask enough questions until you have complete figures and can decide if the bottom line is clear, and affordable. It is equally important to have an idea of the many variables which can affect overall costs. Costs vary by:

Location:

Programs in Western Europe tend to be more expensive than those in most other parts of the world (e.g., Eastern Europe, Africa, Asia, or South America). But relatively expensive programs sometime exist in countries where the cost of living is relatively low, and conversely, depending on the nature of the living and learning experience. The cost of living in countries in which the U.S. Dollar is weak relative to the local currency is (usually) higher than in countries where the U.S. Dollar is strong. Because it costs more to live in most cosmopolitan areas than in the hinterlands, programs based in cities typically cost more.

Sponsor:

In general, programs sponsored by private colleges or organizations are more expensive than those offered by public institutions. If you are interested in a program in a specific location or at a particular foreign university, check to see if more than one sponsor offers it. In some cities, a number of institutions sponsor similar study abroad programs, at a variety of prices.

Program Type:
Island programs, where everything is specially arranged for the U.S. group, are usually more expensive than immersion or direct enrollment programs. Because special or U.S. style services cost more, this is reflected in the program fee. These can include on-site support services, special language-training courses, cross-cultural orientation, social activities, and excursions to sites of interest. The extra expense may be well worth it if this is your first time abroad or you think you would get more out of a program that offers those services. But you can save money by choosing a program that doesn't include them. Remember, however, that you will then have to be more independent when it comes to problem-solving.

Duration:
While some of the costs of participating in a program are the same, regardless of how long the overseas sojourn is (e.g., airfare), other costs vary according to how long one is away, e.g., room and board, tuition, etc. Thus, the longer the program, the more expensive it is, in absolute terms. On the other hand, there are also 'economies of scale,' so that the per week/per credit cost of a summer program may be proportionally greater than the per week/per credit costs of a semester program, etc.

Home Campus Tuition Policy:
Tuition fees at foreign universities, which are usually state supported, are often much lower than those charged by U.S. institutions. Some countries, however, charge separate fees to foreign students that are considerably higher than those charged to local students. If you choose a program sponsored by your own school or another U.S. school, you may find that you're paying full home-campus tuition even if the school you'll be attending abroad charges much lower tuition. The higher cost to you is for the home-campus credit as well as for the home-campus study abroad advising and other administrative and support services.

<u>Financial Aid Availability [see below]</u>
In addition, there are a number of other expenses which may or may not be included in the stated bottom line 'program fee'— and some of which are not part of the 'program' per se, but are nevertheless related to the overall costs of the experience of living and learning in another country. These can include:

General

- Academic Fees
- Application fee (Q: Is it refundable?)
- Administrative fee
- Tuition and other academic fees
- Books and other supplies
- Use of labs and libraries
- Computers: Internet use fees, access to e-mail

Room and Board (Q: Are room and board included during vacations and holidays?)
- Accommodations/Food

- Housing or key deposits
- Residence permits
- Food (Q: Does this include three meals a day? Seven days a week, or weekdays only?)

Transportation

- Round-trip transportation from the United States to the host country
- Transportation between point of international entry and program site, if not included in the round-trip transportation fee
- Commuting costs to and from campus
- Program-related travel
- Optional travel

Travel Documents

- Passport fee
- Visa, if required
- Immunizations, if required
- International Student Identity Card

Insurance

- Health and accident insurance
- Traveler's insurance, for lost or stolen personal items

Miscellaneous

- Admission to cultural sites and events
- Gifts
- Fluctuating exchange rates
- Postage and phone calls

Personal

- Laundry
- Dry cleaning
- Personal care products
- In addition, don't forget to budget money for clothing appropriate to the climate and luggage or a backpack.

Always contact the sponsor directly for the most current information on costs. Exchange rates fluctuate, and the mix of services provided for the program fee can change, so the cost listed in last year's catalog or study abroad guide may no longer be accurate.

FINANCIAL AID

Is Financial Aid Available for Study Abroad?

If you are currently receiving financial aid for your college education, in many cases you can use it to study abroad. This can be the case with aid from an institution, a foundation, the state or federal government, or other private or public sources. Talk to your study abroad advisor, financial aid officer, or bursar about what can and can't be applied to a program of study abroad.

The Higher Education Act (HEA) of 1992 mandated that a student can receive financial aid for study abroad if the student is enrolled in a program approved by the home institution.

Moreover, the student would be eligible to receive "grants, loans, or work assistance without regard to whether the study abroad program is required as a part of the student's degree."

What Types of Financial Aid are Available?

Federal and state governments, foundations, and private and public organizations are primary sources of financial aid. Be sure to check with your financial aid director, study abroad advisor or bursar about whether your financial aid can apply to study abroad.

If you are planning to attend an overseas study program sponsored by another institution, the home institution, through a written agreement between the schools, might allow you to use your financial aid. But students should realize that policies vary among institutions of higher education and therefore, should check with their study abroad advisors and financial aid administrators regarding enrollments with another institution.

Note the following types of financial aid:

Federal Aid

Federal aid can consist of loans, grants, scholarships, or work-study.

Loans:

The Federal Direct Ford Student Loan or the Federal Stafford Guaranteed Student Loan is available to students who demonstrate need. The Federal government pays interest on subsidized loans as long as the student is enrolled half-time and demonstrates financial need through the submission of the Free Application for Federal Student Aid (FAFSA). Repayment begins after you graduate, leave school, or drop below half-time.

These loans can also be unsubsidized and are available to students regardless of need; interest is charged to the students while in school. A student may choose to make the interest-only payments on the unsubsidized loan or allow the interest to be added to the loan principal and then pay both principal and interest after leaving school.

Federal PLUS loans are available to parents of dependent students under the Federal Direct Loan Program and the Federal Family Education Loan Program (FFELP). These loans are made either by the school (direct loan) or through a private lender. Parents are responsible for all interest charges. Repayment begins 60 days after loan disbursements.

Grants and Scholarships:

Federal Pell Grants are awarded to exceptionally needy undergraduate students. Part-time enrollment reduces eligibility.

Federal Supplemental Educational Grants (SEOG) are awarded to exceptionally needy undergraduate students. Must be enrolled at least half-time.

The National Security Education Program (NSEP) and the Fulbright Program funded by the Federal government have grants and fellowships for undergraduate and graduate students for study and research overseas.

Students should be aware that government organizations in other countries such as the German Academic Exchange Service (DAAD) offer funding opportunities.

State Aid

A few states offer assistance to students to attend college which comes from sources other than Federal funding. This aid can be applied to study abroad. It can be need-based or merit based. These include grants or loans but may include tuition waivers, work programs, or other types of aid. The HEA of 1998 stated in the Special Leverage Educational Assistance Partnership Program that "incentive grants are available to States from the Federal government to assist eligible students enrolled in study abroad programs that were approved for credit by the home institution."

Institutional Aid

Some financial aid is funded by the student's home institution, not based on public monies. These scholarships can be based on need and/or on merit. Institutional aid can come from a variety of sources, which includes alumni, faculty, endowments, etc. Some aid can be specified for overseas study but other scholarships can be restricted to the campus, state, or for domestic programs, etc.

If you are planning to attend an overseas study program sponsored by another institution, your home institution, through a written agreement between the schools, might allow you to use your financial aid. But students should realize that policies vary among institutions of higher education and therefore, should check with their study abroad advisors and financial aid administrators regarding enrollments with another institution.

Private and Public Organizations

Other than governmental and institutional aid, private organizations, foundations, corporations, and civic groups are additional sources of aid for study abroad. For example, the Coca-Cola Foundation, Amoco, Chrysler Corporation, etc., have given funds for overseas study. The Rotary Foundation, which has a private, sponsored International scholarship program provides funds for undergraduate, graduate, and vocational students. Some private and public organizations will give overseas study funding for students in a particular major or area of study. Private organizations and associations related to your area of study or destination are worth consulting, as are ethnic and service organizations in your home town. The League of United Latin American Citizens, Alliance Francaise, Dante Alighieri, Goethe groups, etc., are examples of other sources of funding for overseas study and research.

Program Sponsors

Organizations like the American Institute of Foreign Study (AIFS), Syracuse University, Council on International Educational Exchange (CIEE), etc. offer need and merit scholarships for their own sponsored programs. This is, effectively, a form of discounting. Check *Academic Abroad* and *Short Term Study Abroad* published by the Institute of International Education for study abroad programs which offer scholarships or work-study assistance.

Underrepresented Students (Minorities, Students with Disabilities, and Non-Traditional Students)

Various types of financial aid might apply to assist underrepresented students enrolling in overseas study programs. Special grants or scholarships are specified for this purpose. The Robert Bailey Minority scholarships sponsored by the Council of Educational Exchange (CIEE) is a prime example.

Since the passage of the Americans with Disabilities Act in 1990, study abroad and financial aid offices are required to offer the same services to non-disabled and disabled students.

How Do I Make Arrangements to Have Financial Aid Applied to a Study Abroad Program?

Upon application to a study abroad program, you should also contact the financial aid office to see if there are special application processes or policies required in receiving financial aid for overseas study. For example, the study abroad office may provide the financial aid office with costs or a budget for your study abroad program that will facilitate the disbursement of aid when you leave the country. You may also need to check with the bursar's office on how they can contact you or to make financial aid disbursement arrangements. If you have previous loans, you should check wih the registrar's office regarding deferment procedures while you're enrolled overseas. Be sure to check with all four offices, weeks before your plans are finalized. Keep records of all forms submitted and submission dates as well as all personal contacts made (individuals and dates of those contacts). Those records will help you avoid confusion as well as clarify issues that might arise.

Could Financial Aid for Study Abroad Affect Funding for Next Semester's Aid?

There is a possibility that funding for future semesters might be affected resulting from financial aid given for a semester's study abroad program as your eligibility for certain types of aid might have expired. The financial aid office will be monitoring your progress toward your degree as to whether you have exceeded your eligibility requirements. The best advice is to check with a Financial Aid advisor about your funding.

How Many Credits Do I Need to Receive Financial Aid (Including Loans) for Study Abroad?

Credit level required for direct subsidized/unsubsidized loan eligibility for all semesters is half-time time. For undergraduates, half-time requires enrollment in at least 6 credit hours. For scholarships and grants, you need to maintain the enrollment level required for each aid program listed on your financial aid award letter.

Is Power of Attorney Useful if I am Overseas?

If you are overseas, power of attorney gives the designated person (family member or trusted friend); the power to act in your behalf if a legal document requires a signature. If you are receiving federal financial aid, you must endorse the check before it can be deposited. A power of attorney can facilitate the process of receiving funds.

What Sources are Available to Obtain Further Information on Financial Aid and Funding for Study Abroad?

The following on-line and publication sources are very useful for students who wish further information.

ON-LINE INFORMATION

www.finaid.org The Financial Aid Page: links to scholarship searches and comprehensive listing of financial aid information.

www.ed.gov/offices/OSFAP/Students A more comprehensive federal site.

www.ed.gov/proginfo/SFA/StudentGuide The Student Guide: Department of Education publishes a guide each year on the eligibility requirements on various federal aid programs.

http://www.fastweb.com Fast Web. This service provides a free customized list of financial aid sources including private sector scholarships, fellowships, grants, and loans.

www.collegeboard.com College Board Scholarship Search and *www.plato.org* P.L.A.T.O. Scholarship Search are other pertinent engines for grant information.

www.collegenet.com/mach25 Another ready guide to a scholarship search.

www.petersons.com Has references to study abroad which the student might find useful.

www.istc.umn.edu/OSAD/scholarship-search.html (University of Minnesota), *www.lib.msu.edu/harris23/grants/grants.htm* (Michigan State University), and *www.studyabroad.com/os/finaid.html* All three of these websites have information on scholarships and grants for study abroad.

Of course, be sure to also check your school's web site for information about their financial aid and study abroad programs.

PUBLICATIONS

A Student's Guide to Scholarships, Grants, and Funding Publications in International Education and Other Disciplines, Michigan State University, Rm.209, Office of International Studies and Programs, East Lansing, Michigan (April 1997) Contains 79 pages of annotated bibliographical information on references and websites.

Other useful sources include:

Scholarships, Fellowships & Grants for Programs Abroad (American Collegiate Service, 1989),

Gail Ann Schlachter, *Directory of Financial Aid for Women,* 1997-1999; *Financial Aid for African Americans,* 1997-1999 (both from San Carlos,California Reference Service Press)

Marie O'Sullivan, ed., *Financial Resources for International Study,* Institute of International Education, New York, (1996)

DIVERSITY

It is an historical fact that the diversity of student backgrounds represented in U.S. higher education has not been reflected fully in the profiles of students studying abroad. American students of rich ethnic or racial heritage, for instance, have not studied abroad in the same proportions as so-called 'traditional' students. Often the reason is strictly economic, but there are other factors as well. Also underrepresented in study abroad participation over the years have been white males, older students, community college students, as well as students majoring in academic and pre-professional areas— such as science, engineering, business, education, architecture, etc. with rigid curricular sequences. Though students from these underrepresented groups still represent only a small percentage of U.S. undergraduates who study abroad, their numbers have increased dramatically in recent years. Today members of all such groups participate in study abroad, going to every region of the world, and many overseas programs and universities make special efforts to ensure that they feel welcome on their programs and in their classrooms.

Minority Students

If you have a strong ethnic or racial minority background, the key to your successful study abroad experience lies in making an informed choice on what you will find overseas, based on full and accurate information. In these regards, the quality of advising available to you on your home campus may or may not be adequate. Your most important questions are likely to concern how you will be received in a foreign country. However encouraging, and informed your study abroad advisor is, probably your best resource will be other students of color or ethnic minorities who have studied abroad. Returned students report a variety of experiences with racial or ethnic prejudice overseas, just as they have a variety of experiences in this country. Some have found that local people were 'only' curious about their race and ethnicity, which, while occasionally annoying, was not a problem that interfered with their primary reasons for living and learning in another country. There said they were willing, when asked, to answer questions, for instances, about their hair, religion, historically black institutions, and many other topics, as long as the questions were asked with genuine curiosity and did not reflect racist attitudes.

Other returnees report having been elated to find that, for the first time in their lives, their skin color or ethnic heritage was not an issue, although there was still the matter of being a foreigner in that particular country. Still others found some active prejudice in their new host country and had to deal with this however possible. No matter the new social climate, however, the majority of returning minority students felt that the overall experience was so important to their education (in the broadest sense) and their development as individuals that almost all argued that the fear of discrimination should not keep someone at home. As one Spelman College student said, "Getting stared at and hearing ourselves described as 'dirty' was a small price to pay for a semester in the studios of Florentine artists."

Picking the Right Country and Program

The unfortunate fact is that nearly every country discriminates against some group of people although the targets vary from country to country and even within different regions of a country. It is here that the study abroad advisor can play an invaluable role. Ask your advisor to identify countries that have a good track record with minorities, remembering that all minority students are not treated the same way in each country. An African American student will not necessarily have the same experience in Spain or the Dominican Republic that a Hispanic student will.

A student must also be open to the experience and avoid saying the American way is better; it is, after all, only different. It is also the case that certain cities and certain campuses and programs in a given country may be more supportive and tolerant than others.

Talk seriously with your advisor about what you are really looking for and what you are willing to experience— how far outside of your comfort zone do you want to step. Your advisor can probably identify countries as well as programs where minority students have had positive experiences. Countries with wide ethnic diversity like Brazil, Costa Rica, South Africa, and England or those, such as Thailand, in which religious and cultural beliefs encourage tolerance of all peoples, may be good choices. However, you should not necessarily automatically rule out those places which are more homogeneous or less tolerant. The real issue is making an informed choice.

Many students select places in spite of knowing that they are likely to encounter some overt or subtle discrimination there. If you are prepared for whatever attitudes exist, you will usually be able to handle it more constructively. The same is true for your parents, who most likely grew up in times less tolerant than today and, as a result, are afraid to send their children into a situation where they could encounter discrimination. You and your study abroad advisor or perhaps the parents of another returned minority student will need to work with your parents so that they will become comfortable with your choice. There are networks of individuals who can help you and your parents will have a better experience.

Your study abroad advisor should be able to tell you about programs that have offered highly positive experiences to minority participants, and— just as importantly — those that haven't. In addition, she or he may be able to put you in touch with other minority students who have studied abroad. The Comittee on Underrepresentation in Education Abroad, part of NAFSA: Association of International Educators has a list of helpful resources, their web site address is: http://www.secussa.nafsa.org/underrepresentation/links.htm. If requested, the North American Office of Lancaster University can provide minority students and their parents with the names and contact numbers for past minority students and their parents. Many programs use returning students, including minorities, as ambassadors, giving out their names as contacts for their programs.

Exploring Your Heritage

Some minority students may wish to study in a country primarily to explore their cultural roots, whether racial, ethnic, or religious. If this applies to you, consult a study abroad advisor about appropriate programs. While most students who choose a country as part of "heritage-seeking" find it a rewarding experience, nearly all report that they were perceived as primarily 'American' by their hosts — a perception which can be devastating if a student is not prepared for this type of seeming rejection in a region previously thought to be "homeland." Being seen primarily as an 'American,' in spite of one's family roots, often occurs not only in African countries for African American students, but also in China, Hong Kong, Vietnam, Japan, Israel, and even Mexico for students with this heritage. Hispanic students who do not speak fluent Spanish or Asian Americans who cannot speak Japanese or Chinese with some fluency may have a harder time on this type of "heritage" study than other students who expect to be seen as a foreigner and not a long lost relative.

Another issue associated with heritage study abroad is that first generation American parents sometimes want their children to rediscover family 'roots' via study abroad, while their daughters or sons may want to go somewhere else entirely. Your study abroad advisor or your academic advisor may be able to help convince such parents otherwise. It is often necessary to use all your "assets" in order to get permission and support to go abroad, no matter what the destination. Some American colleges initiate contact with parents in order to play a supportive and informing role in this decision. One of the reasons for parental hesitancy is often that student is the main English-speaker for the family and is needed to take grandmother to the doctor and provide a bridge to the English speaking world. Nonetheless, the family can be reassured by help from the study abroad advisor.

If you are concerned about being the only non-white student in a study abroad group or perhaps the only 1 or 2 in a group of 100+, look into programs that are sponsored by institutions with sizable minority populations. Traditionally black colleges, such as Spelman and Lincoln, or colleges with a substantial Hispanic student body, such as Pitzer or Scripps, may sponsor study abroad programs, or can direct you to the sponsors of programs that their students use on a regular basis. You could also try to convince friends of color to study abroad with you, but remember that one of the primary goals of study abroad is to make friends in your host country.

There are several special sources of financial aid earmarked for minority students. If you attend a College Fund/UNCF institution or Howard or Hampton, you are eligible for the Luard Fellowship of The English Speaking Union in New York City. This award covers the full cost of an academic year abroad at a British university of your choice. Students can apply in the fall of their sophomore year for their junior year. Three or four grants are given per year. See your study abroad advisor if you attend an eligible school. Lancaster University provides two Fylde College Scholarships each year for minority students. These grants are approximately 700 pounds sterling and can be used to cover the cost of food and other expenses. The Robert Bailey Scholarships are distributed each semester by Council/CIEE to minority students on their own programs. The application dates are in October and April. The grants are approximately $500 - $1000. The College Fund/UNCF runs a program with the Department of Education and the Woodrow Wilson Foundation called "The Institute for International Public Policy." This is a multiple year commitment for a summer institute after the sophomore year, half the costs of study abroad in the junior year, a Woodrow Wilson junior institute in the summer after the junior year, special language training after the senior year or an internship overseas and then a fellowship to cover much of the cost of an MA degree in International Studies at an APSIA institution, like Georgetown, SAIS, Tufts, or Princeton. Applications for this grant are available to sophomores with a 3.25 in the winter of the sophomore year who are African American, Asian American, Hispanic American or Native American. Twenty scholarships are given each year. Minority students have also done extremely well in the National Security Education Program Fellowship competitions (NSEP). African American, Hispanic American and Asian American students have done extremely well in this competition for fellowships to non-traditional study abroad destinations in diverse disciplines, including science and engineering, social sciences and business. See campus NSEP representative for information. Deadline is typically in early February.

SPECIALIZED FINANCIAL AID

Ask your study abroad advisor or financial-aid officer for assistance in locating grants or loans to study abroad. Some foundations offer special minority scholarships that may be used for study abroad. The federal government has aid targeted to "nontraditional" students—those who are underrepresented in study abroad programs. Some study abroad sponsors, in addition to offering scholarships and work-study, offer special grants or are willing to waive fees for minority students in an effort to attract a diverse student group, including students who might not qualify for other types of aid.

A good source for financial aid for Hispanic students is Hispanic Yearbook-Anuario Hispano, published by T.I.Y.M. Publishing Co. You can get more information online at www.catalog.com/favision. This guide lists Hispanic organizations, publications, radio and TV stations, though not specifically for grant-giving purposes. The 1995 edition includes a diskette of 800 financial aid programs for minorities.

STUDENTS WITH DISABILITIES

Finding a Program Which can Accommodate Your Needs

If you are a U.S. student with a disabilities, you need to know that studying abroad remains an option worth exploring. Whether you have a physical or mobility, learning or psychiatric disability, visual or hearing impairment, a wide range of international opportunities may be still be open to you. The passage of the Americans with Disabilities Act in 1990 has sensitized study abroad offices, international exchange programs, and voluntary service projects regarding the need to provide reasonable accommodations to individuals with disabilities who choose to study outside of the United States. Be sure that your advisor and program provider know what accommodations you will need early in the planning process. You may be asked to provide documentation specifying the nature of your disability. Obviously, there are some limiting factors.

Although programs and universities abroad are becoming more aware of the inclusion of students with disabilities, the extent to which accommodations can be provided depends on the nature of the accommodation needs, the general situation in that particular country regarding accessibility and available services, and the creativity and flexibility of the student and staff/faculty in planning for the experience abroad. Programs will try to provide accommodations as necessary, such as more exam time for a student with a learning disability, materials in alternative formats or readers for someone who is blind, interpreters for a deaf participant, or an accessible home-stay for a person who uses a wheelchair. Some schools abroad also can arrange contact between students with disabilities from the U.S. and the host country.

MOBILITY INTERNATIONAL

Mobility International USA / The National Clearinghouse on Disability and Exchange

If you have a disability and would like to study abroad, your advisor may recommend, in addition to exploring your own institution's program, that you contact Mobility International USA (MIUSA). MIUSA is a non-profit organization dedicated to expanding opportunities for people with disabilities in international exchange, leadership development, disability rights training and community service and, in collaboration with the United States Information Agency, coordinates the National Clearinghouse on Disability and Exchange. The Clearinghouse works with international exchange organizations to increase the inclusion of students with disabilities in their international programs and to advise on ways for making their programs accessible. It provides free information and referral to individuals with disabilities who would like to study, volunteer, or work abroad. MIUSA and the Clearinghouse also publish a semi-annual journal, books, videos and brochures with useful information for those with disabilities who are planning international opportunities. Contact MIUSA and the Clearinghouse at:

Mobility International USA/National Clearinghouse On Disability and Exchange
P.O. Box 10767
Eugene, OR 97440
Telephone: 541-343-1284 (voice/TTY) Fax: 541-343-6812
E-mail: clearinghouse@miusa.org
Website: *www.miusa.org*

An excellent reference for students with disabilities who want to study in Europe or Canada is Studying Abroad: A Guide to Accessible University Programs and Facilities for Students with Disabilities. This is available from:
University of New Orleans Training, Resource and Assistive-Technology Center
P.O. Box 1051
New Orleans, LA 70148
Telephone: 504-280-5700
Fax: 504-280-5707
E-mail: GGAGLIAN@UNO.EDU

VOLUNTARY SERVICE PROJECTS

International voluntary service projects are open to qualified students with disabilities. Examples of voluntary service projects could include building homes for families, establishing art and recreation programs for children, or planting gardens in urban areas. In some areas, if you wish you can participate in projects assisting people with disabilities in the host country. For example, you might choose to teach sign language to children who are hearing impaired.

TRAVEL

U.S. airlines are required to accommodate travelers with Disabilities. A publication called New Horizons for Air Travel with a Disability will tell you about your rights. This is available free of charge by contacting:

Department of Transportation Office of Consumer Affairs
400 Seventh Street SW, Room 10454
Washington, DC 20590
Telephone: 202-366-2220 (voice) or 202-755-7687 (TTY)
Email: airconsumer@ost.dot.gov
Web: *www.dot.gov/airconsumer.*

On foreign carriers, accessibility varies. If you plan to travel on a non-U.S. airline, find out what their policy is regarding Individuals with disabilities and let them know what you need well In advance of departure. General travel and accessibility Information is available from:

Society for the Advancement of Travel For the Handicapped (SATH)
347 Fifth Avenue, Suite 610
New York, NY 10016
Telephone: 212-447-7284
Fax: 212-725-8523
Email: sathtravel@aol.com
Web: *www.sath.org*

Organizations for those with Disabilities in the Host Country

Once you've chosen a country, contact organizations there for people with disabilities. They can tell you what conditions are like in their country for people with disabilities. They can also provide practical information, such as a list of housing that is accessible or recommendations for sign language interpreters. The National Clearinghouse on Disability and Exchange can assist in connecting you with these organizations (see contact information listed above).

HOW TO RESEARCH INTERNSHIP, VOLUNTEER AND WORK ABROAD OPPORTUNITIES

Work abroad: The other way to get an education abroad

An increasing number of U.S. students are interested in hands-on experience abroad, either as a way to immerse themselves in the local culture or to prepare for an international career. You can get this experience through:

- An internship
- Participation in a voluntary service project
- Paid work abroad programs
- Teaching English abroad

For credit or not for credit?

A work experience can be offered as an integral part of a study abroad program, in which case academic credit may be built in (if the program is offered by your own college) or may be transferred towards your degree. Study abroad programs that offer work experiences — usually unpaid — charge tuition and give academic credit. Financial aid may be available.

Alternatively, some work abroad programs are not part of a formal study abroad program, so credit is less likely to be granted for them unless you make special arrangements beforehand. Financial aid is usually not available for non-academic programs.

If you're interested in receiving academic credit for a work abroad experience, consult a study abroad advisor for your school's policy on how to get credit for internships and voluntary service projects (sometimes termed experiential learning). Some schools require that a student have an advisor who evaluates their activities abroad. Students keep journals or write reports, and may be interviewed by their advisor after returning home.

Paid or unpaid?

If you prefer to work abroad in a paid job, be aware that you'll need a work permit. Special officially-recognized work exchange programs, listed in the Paid Work Abroad Programs section below, make this relatively easy to arrange in many countries. Working abroad without a work permit could subject you to deportation or heavy fines!

Internships

Internships provide direct experience in the student's major field of study, giving students an opportunity to try out a career. They vary in length from a few months to one year.

These programs are often for students who have completed at least two years of college. Internship placements are developed in close consultation with program administrators or faculty advisors and are tailored to suit each individual student's needs. Interns may be placed abroad at museums, schools, government offices, international organizations, or corporations.

There are three main types of internships:

- Study-internship programs are sponsored by colleges or universities. Many U.S. undergraduates interested in internships opt for these, which offer the largest number and greatest variety of placements abroad. Like other study abroad programs, study-internships charge tuition and give academic credit. Because of the growing popularity of internship programs and the special arrangements they involve, you must apply for a position and begin making arrangements well in advance. You'll also need to be flexible, since programs usually cannot guarantee placement with a specific company or organization. As with other types of programs, be sure to find out about costs, credit, and housing. If you are receiving financial aid, check to make sure you can use it during an internship. IIE's website and its books, *Academic Year Abroad* and *Short Term Study Abroad,* are the best places to find listings of study-internship programs (<u>see box</u>).

- Paid internships are offered through official work exchange programs. A few officially-recognized work-exchange programs can provide placements and work permits for paid internships abroad. See the section on <u>paid work abroad programs</u> (below) for a list of them.

- Internships are also available with an international organization, corporation, or government. Individual international organizations and corporations such as CNN often accept unpaid interns. "International" internships may be located abroad, or may be with international offices based in the U.S. The U.S. Department of State, the diplomatic branch of the U.S. government, offers a large internship program with a formal application process; deadline for their summer internships is November 1!

Outstanding listings of international internships can be found in: *The Directory of International Internships,* published by Michigan State University's Career Services and Placement Office, and *The International Jobs Directory,* published by Impact Publications (see <u>Resources: Publications section</u>).

Initiative is an important quality for a successful internship. You may have to demonstrate that you can handle responsibility before you're assigned to interesting projects.

GUIDE TO INTERNSHIPS ABROAD

IIE's books *Academic Year Abroad* and *Short Term Study Abroad* have indexed listings for internships and voluntary service projects (called "volunteer/service"), practical training, teaching, or research. Look in the books' indexes under "Special Options." Or use these as search terms in IIE's outstanding website, *www.iie.org.*

Voluntary Service Projects

International voluntary service projects offer opportunities to young people from all over the world to live and work together with local people in community development. Not only do you help others, you experience the local lifestyle and learn firsthand about the political and social issues of a region. This could involve building a school in rural Senegal, planting trees in Brazil, or taking care of children in a Russian orphanage. Voluntary service projects are a good opportunity for students interested in a career in nongovernmental organizations (NGOs) or working with developing countries. Voluntary service projects may be sponsored by NGOs, religious organizations, or government organizations such as the Peace Corps.

Often, no special skills are required. Hundreds of short-term voluntary service projects (also known as "workcamps") take place during the summer for two- or three-week periods, but it is also possible to participate in semester or academic-year programs. For graduates, paid long-term volunteering for a period of two years through programs such as the Peace Corps may be an option. Many short-term projects are offered in Europe (and worldwide), with longer-term projects usually taking place in developing countries.

Some study abroad programs incorporate a service project — you pay tuition for a program of coursework combined with volunteering, and get academic credit. IIE's books *Academic Year Abroad* and *Short Term Study Abroad* are good sources for finding "service-learning" study abroad programs.

For other short-term, nonacademic volunteer service projects, the work is usually unpaid but volunteers may receive room and board. Nearly all programs charge fees (from $200 upwards) to partially cover the costs of placing, training, and on-site support of volunteers.

To learn the highs and lows of voluntary service projects that interest you, talk to former participants. Most organizations will provide contact information on students and others who have participated in their programs. A good book on the benefits and challenges of volunteering abroad is How to Serve & Learn Abroad Effectively: Students Tell Students, available from:
The International Partnership for Service-Learning
815 Second Ave - Suite 3155
New York, NY 10017
Telephone: 212-986-0989
Fax: 212-986-5039
Email: <u>pslny@aol.com</u>
Web: *www.ipsl.org*

An excellent directory listing both short- and long-term programs for volunteering abroad is: The Peace Corps and More: 175 Ways to Work, Study and Travel at Home & Abroad, published by Global Exchange (see Resources: Publications section).

To register for short-term volunteer service programs, contact:
VFP (Volunteers for Peace)
1034 Tiffany Road
Belmont, VT 05730-0202
Telephone: 802-259-2759
Fax: 802-259-2922
Email: vfp@vfp.org
Web: *www.vfp.org,* or the CIEE (see next section)

The Peace Corps, a U.S. government-sponsored program offered in over 90 countries, is one of the largest and best-paying volunteer programs, if you are ready to make a two-year commitment and are qualified. Contact:
Peace Corps
Room 8500
1990 K Street NW
Washington, DC 20526
Telephone: 800-424-8580
Web: *www.peacecorps.gov*

Paid Work Abroad Exchange Programs

These programs offer work permits and placements into short-term paid jobs, or on-site assistance in finding them. Programs are usually for a period of a summer or semester, though some offer permits for up to 18 months. Work exchange programs operate on the basis of official reciprocal exchange agreements between the U.S. and foreign governments.

Some of these programs assist with work permits and the on-site job search, while others offer placements. Fees range between $200-1,000. Most participants are able to earn enough to cover their expenses while abroad.

Types of paid jobs available run the gamut from internships to typical summer jobs such as temping and restaurant work. But you're less likely to find paid work in governmental or non-profit sectors and in non-applied fields such as the fine arts or social sciences. Also, work in less-developed countries, if it can be found at all, will pay at local wage rates - a fraction of wages in the U.S.!

AIESEC (from the French acronym for the International Association of Students in Economics & Business Management) is an international student-run organization which offers approximately 5,000 paid internships each year in business and other fields in over 80 countries. Application for AIESEC internships is usually possible only through campus chapters. Contact:
AIESEC-USA
135 West 50th Street, 17th Floor
New York, NY 10020-1202
Telephone: 212-757-3774
Fax: 212-757-4062
E-mail: aiesec@us.aiesec.org
Web: *www.us.aiesec.org*

AIPT (Association for International Practical Training) / IAESTE (International Association for the Exchange of Students for Technical Experience). Contact:
AIPT/IAESTE
10 Corporate Center, Suite 250
10400 Little Patuxent Parkway
Columbia, MD 21044-3510
Telephone: 410-997-2200
Fax 410-992-3924
E-mail: aipt@aipt.org
Web: *http://www.aipt.org*
This non-profit organization offers several different programs:

IAESTE offers engineering & science internships in over 60 countries for students (apply by early December). The Student Exchanges Program offers work permits in numerous countries for students who find their own internships. The Career Development program provides work permits for up to 18 months in Austria (11 month limit), Britain (12 month limit), Finland, France, Germany, Hungary, Ireland, Japan, Malaysia, Mexico, Slovak Republic, Sweden, and Switzerland for university graduates who find their own placements.

American-Scandinavian Foundation - This non-profit organization offers internship placements in Scandinavian countries for students of technical subjects as well as positions in Finland for teaching English or farming. ASF can also assist with short-term work permits in Scandinavian countries for those who have job offers. Contact:
American-Scandinavian Foundation
15 East 65th Street
New York, NY 10021
Telephone: 212-879-9779
Fax: 212-249-3444
Email: training@amscan.org
Web: *www.amscan.org.*

BUNAC (British Universities North American Club), a non-profit organization, offers the Work in Britain program. With 6,000 American participants annually, this is one of the most popular work abroad programs. The program provides a work-permit and job-search assistance, but does not offer job placements. BUNAC's Work in Britain handbook has a large selection of addresses of potential employers. BUNAC also offers a similar Work in Australia program. For students and recent graduates (within one semester of graduation) only. Contact:
BUNAC: Work in Britain & Australia programs
P.O. Box 430
Southbury, CT 06488
Telephone: 800-GO-BUNAC or 203-264-0901
Fax: 203-264-0251
Email: info@bunacusa.org
Web: *http://www.bunac.org*

Camp Counselors USA - This non-profit organization offers several programs for students and non-students: Work in Australia and Work in New Zealand, as well as programs which offer placements to serve as camp counselors in Russia and Venezuela. Contact:
Outbound Program
2330 Marinship Way, Suite 250
Sausalito, CA 94965

Telephone: 1-800-999-2267
Fax: 415-339-2744
Email: outbound@campcounselors.com
Web: *http://www.campcounselors.com*

CDS International - A non-profit organization that offers paid internship programs in Germany for students, graduates and professionals for periods ranging from a summer to a year. CDS can also assist with work permits in Germany for those who have job offers. Contact:
CDS International
871 United Nations Plaza, 15th Floor
New York, NY 10017-1814
Telephone: 212-497-3500
Fax: 212-497-3535
Email: info@cdsintl.org
Web: *http://www.cdsintl.org*

CIEE (Council on International Educational Exchange or COUNCIL Exchanges) - The non-profit Council Work Abroad program, one of the largest work abroad programs (with over 2,000 U.S. participants annually), offers short-term work permits and job search support for France, Germany, Ireland, Canada, Costa Rica, Australia and New Zealand. The Council also offers a Teach in China program and International Volunteer Projects in around 30 countries. Contact:
CIEE
205 East 42nd Street
New York, NY 10017-5706
Telephone: 888-COUNCIL
Email: info@councilexchanges.org
Web: *http://www.ciee.org*

InterExchange - A non-profit organization which offers a variety of placements for students and non-students. Apply four months in advance of desired departure date: English Teaching in Bulgaria, Costa Rica, Czech Republic, Hungary and Poland; internships in Germany for marketing, trade and tourism, museums, and business; farm work in Norway; au pair (child care) placements in Austria, France, Germany, Holland, Italy, Norway, Spain, and Switzerland. Contact:
InterExchange
161 Sixth Avenue
New York, NY 10013
Telephone: 212-924-0446
Fax: 212-924-0575
Email: info@interexchange.org
Web: *http://www.interexchange.org*

International Cooperative Education Program - This program provides around 450 paid summer internships in Switzerland, Germany, Belgium, Finland, Japan, Singapore, Argentina, Brazil or Chile for students and recent graduates who have studied the appropriate language: German, French, Italian, Finnish, Dutch, Japanese, Chinese, Spanish or Portuguese. Apply by January. Contact:
International Cooperative Education Program
15 Spiros Way
Menlo Park, CA 94025

Telephone: 650-323-4944
Fax: 650-323-1104
Email: ICEmenlo@aol.com

TEACHING ENGLISH ABROAD

English has become the language of choice for much of the world when it comes to business, technology, diplomacy and higher education. Because of this, teaching English abroad is an accessible and popular option for paid long-term working abroad - especially for college graduates (a few programs, including ones designed for student teaching, are open to current students). The need for teachers of English is greatest in regions outside of Western Europe.

Several of the programs already mentioned above offer placements for teaching English abroad — AIESEC, the American-Scandinavian Foundation, the CIEE Teach in China program, InterExchange, and the Peace Corps.

Examples of other major programs for teaching English abroad include:

Fulbright English Teaching Assistantships - One-year positions available in Belgium & Luxembourg, France, Germany, Hungary, Korea and Turkey. Bachelor's degree required; strong preference is given to majors in appropriate foreign language who intend to be future teachers. Application deadline is in mid-September a year before the position starts. Contact:
Fulbright English Teaching Assistantships
U.S. Student Programs Division
Institute of International Education
809 United Nations Plaza
New York, NY 10017-3580
Telephone: 212-984-5330

JET Program - Sponsored by the Japanese government, this program offers placements for teaching English in junior or senior high schools in Japan for one year. Several thousand positions available each year. Bachelor's degree and U.S. citizenship required. Application deadline is in early December. Also, for those with at least intermediate command of Japanese, Coordinator of International Relations positions are available. Contact:
Office of the JET Program
Embassy of Japan
2520 Massachusetts Ave, NW
Washington, DC 20008
Telephone: 202-238-6772, 202-238-6773 or toll-free 800-INFO-JET
Web: www.jet.org or www.mofa.go.jp/j_info/visit/jet/index.html

How to find out more about working abroad and international careers The magazine Transitions Abroad is the only U.S. publication which regularly publishes first-hand reports about work abroad - see if your college's study abroad office carries it. For listings of many more work abroad programs than we have room for here, along with some of the best articles from Transitions Abroad, get their book, *Work Abroad: The Complete Guide to Finding a Job Overseas,* Clay Hubbs, editor, 1999. Contact:
Transitions Abroad
P.O. Box 1300
Amherst, MA 01004
Telephone: 800-293-0373
Fax: 413-256-0373
Email: info@transitionsabroad.com
Web: www.transitionsabroad.com

For books about long-term international careers, we especially recommend the International Jobs Directory, by Ron and Caryl Krannich, 1999, Impact Publications, and International Jobs: Where They Are, How to Get Them, by Eric Kocher and Nina Segal, 1999, Perseus Books. These and many other international job resources can be ordered from:

Impact Publications
9104-N Manassas Drive
Manassas Park, VA 20111-5211
Telephone: 800-361-1055
Fax: 703-335-9486
Web: *www.impactpublications.com.*

Websites for Work Abroad and International Careers These are good sites to start with, and are far better than a random search of the web. Each site provide links to many, many more sites and programs specifically about working abroad.

www.goabroad.com, GoAbroad.com

www.iie.org, Institute of International Education

http://teach.studyabroad.com/exp.html, StudyAbroad.com

http://www.transitionsabroad.com, Transitions Abroad magazine

http://www.cie.uci.edu/~cie/iop, University of California-Irvine, International Opportunities Program

http://www.umich.edu/~icenter/overseas, University of Michigan, International Center

http://www.istc.umn.edu, University of Minnesota, International Study and Travel Center (ISTC)

http://internationaleducation.wlv.edu/workabroad/ Washington and Lee University, Office of International Education

PART III: BEFORE YOU LEAVE HOME

Once you have been accepted into a study abroad program, you must next pay serious attention to the details of preparing to go abroad. Just as you did when you chose what to study and where, give yourself plenty of time to make all of the many necessary pre-departure arrangements.

The better prepared you are for your study abroad experience — the more you know about what to expect and what is expected of you- the more meaningful your experience will be. It should go without saying that you should try to learn as much as you can about your host country — its language, history and culture as well as its current social and political conditions. There are many ways to do this: take courses, read books and magazine articles, surf the Web, talk with people from there and who've been there, etc. As Socrates said, "The innocent eye sees nothing."

This section will advise you on a host of essential matters which must be taken care of before you leave. Note: Some of the following information might also be provided by your campus, or the host program, or overseas institution.

PRE-DEPARTURE ORIENTATION

If your home school is the program sponsor, you will probably have a pre-departure orientation on campus. If not, then you should at least receive orientation information through the mail, on the phone or via the Internet.

Orientations and orientation materials usually cover the following topics:

- Travel documents (passport, visa, etc.)
- Travel arrangements (international transportation, etc.)
- Housing information (living arrangements, roommates, etc.)
- Health and safety issues (what to do, what not to do)
- Financial matters (payments schedules, financial aid, etc.)
- Communication with family and friends (how to establish, etc.)
- Host culture information (history, customs, laws, politics, etc.)
- Knowledge of home culture (what others will see in your 'Americanness')

THE BELOW SUMMARY MAY OR MAY NOT REPEAT WHAT YOU OTHERWISE WILL BE TOLD:

Travel Documents

When traveling outside the United States, you need to carry a passport, the only form of identification recognized everywhere which verifies your citizenship. Depending on the length of stay, there are a few areas of the world such as Canada, Mexico and some Caribbean countries that allow U.S. citizens entry without a passport. However, a valid passport is always the best form of identification. Some countries will also require an additional entry document called a visa. Passports are issued by your country of citizenship, while visas — usually a stamp on a page of the passport, though they can be a separate certificate — are issued by the country to be visited.

Passport

Apply early for a passport. The normal processing time is four to six weeks — even longer during the peak travel season (March to August). If you have never had a passport, you may apply to a passport agent at a U.S. Department of State agency. You can also make application through selected post offices or clerks of any federal, state or county courthouse. If you have a passport already but it will expire during the time you are abroad, apply for a new one before you leave. You must apply in person unless you are renewing a passport obtained after you were eighteen.

HERE IS A LIST OF WHAT YOU MUST PRESENT ALONG WITH YOUR APPLICATION FORM:

- Proof of U.S. citizenship (an official birth certificate, a naturalization certificate, or a previous U.S. passport)
- Two recent identical color photographs (2"x2") with a white background
- Form of current identification with your signature and photograph (i.e., a driver's license)
- $60.00 fee if you are eighteen years or older, $40.00 if you are younger

Make several photocopies of your passport. Leave a copy at home with your family and carry a copy with you at all times when you are overseas. Be sure to keep an additional copy with your belongings. If you should lose your passport, the copies may speed up the process of replacing it. If this happens, immediately notify the nearest U.S. embassy or consulate.

You can get more information about passports on line at *http://travel.state.gov/passport_services.html* or by calling National Passport Information Center at (900) 255-5674.

VISA

Some countries require that U.S. citizens have a visa, depending on the length and purpose of their stay. A visa is an official document giving permission to enter a country and is granted by the government of the country you wish to enter. it may be in the form of a stamp imprinted on a page in your passport or it might be an official document which includes a photograph.

Visa requirements vary from country to country. Information relating to all visas may be obtained from the nearest embassy or consulate of the country or countries in which you will study and/or travel. An on-line source is *http://travel.state.gov/foreignentryreqs.html.* If you are planning to study in a country for an extended period of time, you may need a student visa or residency permit. In most cases, you will need to get the visa before leaving the United States. Check with your program sponsor to see what the requirements are. They may need to provide special letters or documents that must accompany your visa application. Note that you may also need passport-size photos. It's a good idea to have extra copies of these photos for this purpose and other situations.

INTERNATIONAL STUDENT IDENTITY CARD

Next to your passport and visa, if needed, the International Student Identity Card (ISIC) can be among the most valuable travel documents for you to have. It verifies your student status and it is widely recognized throughout the world. With the card, you are eligible to qualify for discounts ranging from lower airfares, cheaper insurance coverage to reduced or free admission to museums, theaters, concerts and cultural sites around the world.

The ISIC also provides supplemental health insurance coverage. This plan covers emergency medical evacuation in case your illness or injury cannot be treated overseas and repatriation of remains in case of death. Most private health care plans do not incorporate this kind of coverage. This is why many program sponsors are either providing a special overseas insurance plan or requiring the card.

Not only do you receive the medical coverage and discounts while overseas, but you also have access to a toll-free help line for assistance with medical, legal, or financial emergencies. In addition, you can use the card in the United States for special student discounts on airlines, lodging, international phone calls and international money transfers. The card comes with a detailed hand book that provides information on all its uses.

The card is issued by the Council on International Educational Exchange (Council). It is available at all Council Travel Offices and is also sold at many U.S. colleges and universities. Check with your study abroad office to see if it is sold there. You can also order it from:
Council
205 East 42nd Street
New York, NY 10017
Phone: 1-888-COUNCIL

MAKING TRAVEL AND HOUSING ARRANGEMENTS

Many study abroad programs take care of participants' international travel and housing arrangements. If this is not the case with your program, then it will be your responsibility to arrange for travel to your program site and/or find your own accommodations. You may also want to consider making plans for your own transportation and housing if you decide to do additional traveling at the end of your program.

Housing

If housing is not provided for you by your study abroad program, give yourself plenty of time to arrange for it. Since student housing is at a premium in most countries, ask for housing recommendations from a representative from your program. If you are enrolling directly in a foreign university, contact the university to see if there is a student housing office which can assist you in your search for accommodation.

Air Transportation

Some program sponsors include group flights to and from the program site. Others require you to make your own arrangements. If you do need to arrange your own transportation, be sure to do so well in advance of leaving, especially if you plan to travel during the summer or any other period when air travel is heavy. Make sure you know what arrangements have been made for the arrival of students in your host country before finalizing your flight reservations. Often a designated meeting place and time are established so that program staff can greet students upon their arrival. Many countries list a round-trip ticket as one of their entry requirements.

Even though you may not know when you want to return home and you may have to pay a surcharge to change your return ticket; it is still cheaper to buy the round-trip ticket instead of buying two one-way tickets. Shop carefully to find a flight that best suits your needs. Compare the price of open-ended tickets, in which you return at any point within a specified length of time, with the price of a ticket bearing a stated return date. If you are planning to travel on your own after your program ends, you might want to investigate "open jaw" fares, which let you return from a different location from your point of arrival.

Council Travel is an excellent source of information about student travel. It publishes the Student Travels magazine which is distributed free to over 1,000 colleges and universities in the United States. With your International Student Identity Card, you can sometimes get up to 50% off of commercial airfares through Council Travel. More information about Council and its travel services is available on-line at www.ciee.org. Another student travel agency offering airfare discounts is STA Travel at the following address:
STA Travel
7202 Melrose Avenue
Los Angeles, CA 9004
Information is also available on-line at www.statravel.org. Free travel literature is usually available from the government tourist office, consulate or embassy of the country or countries to which you travel. You can also learn more about discount airfares from the following websites:

www.budgettravel.com/

www.routesinternational.com (provides links to airlines)

www.travelocity.com among many, many others

If you lose your airline ticket, contact the airline, travel agency, or other agency from which you purchased the ticket. If you bought your ticket from an airline, you will have to fill out a claim for a lost ticket and buy a new ticket. You'll be refunded the cost of the replacement ticket, minus a fee. The fee varies with each airline. It takes about six months to get your refund. If you purchased Student Tickets, issued by STA Travel and other agencies, you don't need to buy a new ticket; you simply pay a $25 fee and your ticket will be reissued.

Don't buy a one-way ticket, even if you don't know when you want to return home. Most foreign countries require visitors to have a round-trip ticket before they are allowed to enter.

Rail Passes

In many countries, rail travel is probably the most widely used mode of transportation. Buying a rail-pass in the United States prior to your departure can greatly reduce your costs. Rail passes, such as the Britrail Pass or Eurail Pass, can be obtained from most travel agents. These passes usually offer unlimited travel for a specific amount of time. Just as there are special airfares for students, there are also special rail passes for students.
Website: www.raileurope.com

Travel by Car

If you are planning to travel by car, be aware that renting a car abroad and filling it with gasoline can be quite expensive. Just as in the United States, each country requires you to have a valid driver's license. Some countries will recognize your current U.S. driver's license. Others may require you to obtain an International Driver's Permit. Contact your local AAA (American Automobile Association) Office or the
AAA National Headquarters
8111 Gatehouse Road
Falls Church, VA 22042

Remember also that other countries have different "rules of the road." Prior to departure, you may also wish get some information on international road travel. One source is:
The Association for Safe International Road Travel
5413 West Cedar Lane, Suite 103C
Bethesda, MD 20814
301-983-5252
Email: asisrt@erols.com
Website: *www.asirt.org*

Make sure that you also check to see if your U.S. automobile insurance covers you and rental cars overseas.

Travel Light

Aim to travel light. Keep in mind that, for most international flights, you are allowed to check only two pieces of luggage. Some airlines have restrictions for the weight of each piece of luggage; check before you pack. If your program is a study-tour, you will have to carry whatever you bring, so restrict yourself to one or two moderate-sized bags and a small carry-on bag in which to keep valuables, passport, and camera equipment.

Insure your baggage and personal effects for the full period abroad. If you bring a camera, buy a lead-lined film bag. Contrary to posted airport claims, some X-ray devices ruin film.

Youth Hostels

When traveling on weekends, during school breaks or at the end of your study abroad experience, you may want to consider staying in a youth hostel. Hostels are much cheaper than hotels and can range from dormitory-style room to private rooms. They may have restrictions. For example, they may impose curfews, require you to bring your own bedding or limit your stay to a certain number of nights.

In order to stay in hostels, you may be required to have an International Youth Hostel Pass, another form to obtain before your departure. The pass and a handbook with locations and contact information are available from:
Hosteling International/American Youth Hostels
National Office
P.O. Box 37613
Room 804
Washington, DC 20013-7613
Phone: 1-800-444-6111

Many countries also have student hostels, which are restricted to use by university students. These usually offer more conveniences than youth hostels, such as food service, and are a great way to meet other international students. You may need to have a valid International Student Identity Card to prove your student status. Lastly, some independent hostels exist, open to students as well as to other travelers.

Other Accommodations

Other options for accommodations when you travel are bed-and-breakfasts, pensions, and budget hotels. Talk to your travel advisor before departure about budget accommodations at your travel destinations. You can also browse the travel section of a local bookstore for travel guidebooks aimed at college students.

VISIT TRAVEL WEBSITES

You can find out more about travel abroad online. For information on cheap accommodations, visit:

www.hostels.com

www.travlang.com/hotels

For information on discounted travel by plane, train, bus, and ferry, visit:

www.transitionsabroad.com/listings/travel/index.shtml

www.istc.umn.edu/html/trav_prod.html

http://www.statravel.com (Council Travel Centers worldwide)

www.routesinternational.com (links to airlines, trains, ferries, and buses)

www.etn.nl (European Travel Networks discounts in 185 countries)

www.budgettravel.com

PREPARATION FOR HANDLING BUSINESS AT HOME WHILE OVERSEAS

While you are overseas, you will need to take care of certain civil, financial and legal matters in the United States. Advance planning in these areas will make life easier.

Power of Attorney

Giving a family member or trusted friend power of attorney, while you are abroad, is a good idea. Power of attorney gives that designated person the power to act on your behalf in case a legal document requires your signature while you are away. This is especially important if you receive financial aid. Checks that you receive to cover educational costs must be endorsed by you before they can be deposited. It may also be helpful when completing and signing other financial aid forms, such as your FAFSA (Free Application for Student Aid), that must be taken care of while you are gone. Check with the student legal services office on your campus to obtain this document. You can also give someone power of attorney by simply writing what duties that person will be allowed to perform on your behalf and having the paper notarized.

Absentee Voting

If elections are going to take place in the United States while you are overseas, you can still take part in the election process by completing an absentee ballot. You must, however, register to vote before you leave home. Contact local election officials to obtain information on absentee voting, including whether you need to have your ballot notarized at a U.S. embassy or consulate.

Filing Income Tax

If you currently pay income tax and will be out of the United States during spring semester, you can request an extension of the deadline for filing federal, state and local tax returns. If you choose to file from abroad, then you can request your family or friends to send you the necessary paperwork. You can also find out if the closest American embassy or consulate has forms. The embassy and consulate staff may also be able to find someone to help you complete the forms.

U.S. Customs and Duties

If you plan on taking expensive items, such as cameras, Walkmans, CD players, personal computers, etc., you should consider registering them with U.S. Customs before you leave. That way those items won't be subject to duty when you return. Save receipts for major purchases made overseas, as you may be able to get reimbursed for the taxes (VAT) paid. You are allowed to bring up to $400.00 of gifts and souvenirs duty free. Above that amount, you will be charged an import duty equivalent to ten percent of the value of the items. A good publication to get before you leave is "Know Before You Go" which can be obtained from the U.S. Customs Office.

Pre-Arranging Money Matters

The major costs of your study abroad program (tuition and fees, housing, sometimes food and occasionally international airfare) are usually billed and paid prior to departure to the sponsoring institution. Be sure you know exactly what is covered and what is not covered in those costs so that you are prepared to cover all other expenses. It is a good idea to make a weekly budget and then live by it so you don't run out of money and have no quick way to replace it.

Currency Exchange

Traveling with large amounts of cash is not recommended. You should consider using several different forms of payment for your expenses. Traveler's checks, credit cards, ATM cards and cash can all be used effectively depending on the country.

You can obtain traveler's checks in U.S. dollars and some foreign currencies at most banks and travel agencies. Some of the companies that offer traveler's checks are American Express, Citicorp, Thomas Cook, etc. It is best to get the checks in $100.00, $50.00, and $20.00 denominations. That way you can regulate the amount of money you want rather than changing huge denomination checks. Traveler's checks can be replaced if lost so it is important to keep the serial number list separate from the actual checks.

It is always good to have some local currency when you arrive on site. Exchange some U.S. dollars upon arrival at the international arrival airport where the exchange rates and fees are better than at the departing U.S. airport. Later on in your experience, it is recommended that you exchange your money at the major national banks throughout the world. Railroad stations in Europe are also recommended spots. The banks and their ATM machines usually offer the fairest exchange rate but you will pay a commission fee each time.

Credit and Bank Cards

Credit cards can be used to get foreign currency at a good rate of exchange and are invaluable if an emergency arises. They are widely accepted in most places in most countries, although some countries will only allow cash for financial transactions. The three main cards are American Express, Visa and Master Card, although American Express is less common in most student settings. A debit/check card is also recommended. Check before you leave to be sure that your PIN can be used overseas. If not, then you will need to get a new one.

Setting up Communications with Family and Friends

You and your family and friends need to decide what the best means of communication will be — mail, telephone, or e-mail. Each has its own merits as well as some disadvantages.

Mail

Sending letters back and forth can take a long time, usually more than a week for an airmail letter to leave the States, arrive at the host country and then to reach you at the local site. International postage is more expensive than domestic postage; but if you keep it to letters or postcards, it won't cost too much. Mailing packages by surface mail is less expensive than by air mail, but allow a lot of time. Don't forget your address book! Your family and friends will love getting postcards from you. And you will be delighted to go to your mailbox to find a letter or package from home. Finally, your letters home make a wonderful collection of memories for you when you return.

Make a photocopy of your address book and keep it separate from the original. That way if you lose your address book, you'll still be able to keep in touch with people.

Telephone and Fax

There's nothing quite like calling home to talk with your family and friends or receiving a phone call from them. However, it can be quite expensive for both sides. You can now dial an international call directly from the United States for less than an operator-assisted call. Check out the special deals always being offered by the long-distance carriers. Dialing direct from overseas to your home is also possible, especially with a phone card. Again, check the U.S. long-distance carriers about getting a phone card before you leave. When calling, don't forget the time difference! A time that might be convenient for you may not be convenient for your family and friends.

AT&T Direct Service, Sprint, and MCI, as well as many other telephone companies, offer easy and sometimes inexpensive ways to call home. Check with your service for a list of access numbers for nearly every country. All you have to do is call the access number for the country you are calling from, then dial the phone number you're calling and your calling card number. Typically there will be an English-speaking operator, so you don't need to worry if your command of the local language is still rudimentary.

Remember to remind the people at home that you may not have a phone immediately available. As a result you may not be able to phone them as soon as you arrive. Agree on a time by which you definitely will have called home.

Phone Tips

If you need to make more than one call, don't hang up after each one; press # and you can avoid separate access charges for each call. If you press a wrong number, don't hang up, press the * key; this will allow you to start over. Remember the time difference between your country and the part of the United States you want to call. As in the United States, shield the phone keypad when entering your calling card number so no one can see it and use it. In countries where touch-tone service is not available, your long distance company may have voice-activated service and dialing.

Faxing mail and other documents home is a good alternative, as long as there is easy access to a fax machine at each end. Faxing is cheaper than long distance phone charges, but far more expensive than e-mail. Faxing gets around time zone disparities, meaning that what is sent can be read at the other end whenever it is convenient, which may not be when it arrives.

E-mail

E-mail has become the main mode of communication, both domestically and internationally. It eliminates the time difference inconvenience and it is much less expensive than phoning. However, it only works if the U.S.-based family and friends and the student overseas have similar access to the Internet. E-mail is great to have as it saves time when dealing with practical matters such as getting new course approvals for a switched class or for relaying campus information to students. It also means immediate contact when an emergency arises. However, you must avoid the temptation to sit at your computer all day instead of exploring daily life in your host country. Set a limit for yourself and stick to it. Don't let your real experience become a virtual study abroad.

Planning for Overseas Health

Your health and safety during your study abroad experience will depend on the choices you make and precautions that you take prior, during, and following your time overseas. However, there are no guarantees or absolutes with regard to health and safety in any setting, especially an international one. Before your departure, make sure that you are in good health, get any immunizations that are required and learn as much as you can about the health and safety conditions in your host country. Many study abroad programs sponsors will require you to submit medical forms about your physical and mental health. You will also be asked to show proof of health and accident insurance or you may be asked to purchase a special policy that covers these areas overseas. More discussion of these topics should be a part of your on-site orientation.

Regular Checkups

Be sure to have a physical and dental checkup before you go, especially if you will be gone at a time when you would normally schedule these appointments and/or your will be studying in a developing country. This will give you an opportunity to talk with your health care professionals about any general health precautions you should take.

Pre-existing Conditions

If you have an ongoing medical problem, such as allergies or diabetes, you need to take special precautions in preparing for and managing your condition overseas. How will the stresses of the environment and the study abroad experience impact your health? If you have a disability, how will your needs be met?

Prescriptions

If you take prescription medications regularly, bring a supply to last throughout your time abroad, if practical. Foreign drugs are not necessarily closely related to those standard in the United States, even if they have the same chemical formula. They may be marketed under different names and may not be available in the strengths you desire. It might be wise to also have a letter from your home physician or pharmacist describing your medicines, their dosage, a generic name for them and describing the condition being treated. This letter could be helpful in an emergency.

Make sure all drugs are in the original pharmacy containers and are clearly labeled. You should carry copies of the prescriptions to avoid problems with Customs. In the case of narcotic medicines, it may not be prudent to carry additional supplies because of possible Customs difficulties. In that case, bring a prescription with the drug's generic name.

If you are diabetic or have another medical condition in which a syringe is needed to administer medication, bring a supply of disposable syringes. These are not available in all countries, and are essential to protect yourself against HIV, hepatitis, and other communicable illnesses. Even if you don't routinely inject medication, it's a good idea to bring a few disposable syringes if you will be studying in a country where they are not available, in the event that you need an injection. Some countries, however, restrict the import of syringes — as well as certain medications and contraceptives. Before departure, find out of this applies to your host country.

For certain conditions such as diabetes, asthma, mild epilepsy, or allergy to penicillin, it would be wise to wear a tag or a bracelet or carry a card to identify the condition so that the student can be treated properly. Take an extra pair of eyeglasses and/or contact lenses if you wear them. Bring along extra contact lens solution too. Do not pack your medications in your checked luggage. Pack them in your carry on so as not to be without them if your luggage gets lost.

For the flight to your program site, put any prescription medication, eyeglasses, and contact lenses in your carry-on bag. Don't take the risk of these items being misrouted or lost with your checked luggage.

World and Regional Health Conditions

Some health problems, such as diarrhea, are worldwide; whereas, some diseases like malaria are found only in certain regions. The CDC (Centers for Disease Control) and the U.S. State Department's Overseas Citizens Emergency Center can give you detailed information about particular regions you plan to visit on study abroad.

Centers for Disease Control
www.cdc.gov
1-800-311-3435

Overseas Citizens Emergency Center
(202) 647-5225

Additional information about health issues abroad is available from:
American College Health Association
15879 Crabbs Branch Way
Rockville, MD 20855

Many travelers experience some form of diarrhea while adjusting to local food and water. In many cases, it is mild but ask your doctor to recommend an anti-diarrhea medication so you can take it with you. If you are going to a country in a tropical region where there may be bacterial, fungal and parasitic diseases, be sure you get some anti-malarial medication. Your doctor may recommend that you start taking it before you leave the United States. One can also contract hepatitis or cholera in countries where the drinking water is untreated. Students must take preventative measures and receive treatment if necessary.

Sexually-transmitted diseases (STDs), such as gonorrhea, syphilis, and herpes, pose health risks in any country. The HIV virus, from which AIDS is contracted, can be transmitted sexually but also through contaminated hypodermic needles and blood supplies. If you are going to a country where AIDS is prevalent, find out what you should do in an emergency if you require an injection or a blood transfusion.

Immunizations

While some countries require immunizations for a visa or entry, others do not. These requirements can change according to the health conditions of a particular country. Therefore, it is important to check on a regular basis to see if your host country has requirements. Check also to see if your country requires an AIDS test for entry or the residency permit. Even if immunizations are not required, you still may want to get them. Be sure to discuss this with your doctor, local travel clinic or county health department. If you will travel to other countries, don't forget to check their immunization requirements, as well.

You may be required to present an official record of immunizations. An "International Certificate of Vaccinations" is the most common form used. It is issued by the U.S. Department of Health and Human Services and is approved by the World Health Organization. You can get the form from your local department of health, travel clinic, passport offices and from many physicians and travel agencies. It must be filled out and dated by the person who provides the immunization. Your campus health service may be able to provide the form and the necessary immunizations.

It may be also wise for you to have your basic childhood immunizations (tetanus, polio, diphtheria, etc.) updated. If you will be traveling to a developing country, then typhoid fever, hepatitis A and B, cholera and yellow fever are frequently recommended immunizations. Don't forget anti-malarial medicine if traveling to malarial areas.

Substance Abuse

Substance abuse is viewed differently around the world. Sometimes students who are away from their home campuses and the U.S. laws regarding the use of alcohol, fall into patterns of alcohol abuse. They may misinterpret how alcohol is used in their new culture. It may be less expensive to buy; there may be a lower drinking age or maybe the laws against drunkenness are less stringent. Your program sponsors will most likely discuss this topic during your orientation to explain the program's regulations concerning alcohol consumption as well as the consequences for abuse. If you currently attend a support group such as Alcoholics Anonymous, check on meeting availability and schedules in your host country. (For Alcoholics Anonymous contact Alcoholics Anonymous World Services, Telephone: 212-870-3400).

Drug abuse can lead to immeasurable health risks as well as serious cultural and legal consequences. Risks are magnified tenfold by impure drugs, shady and often criminal contacts, and rigid legal systems that impose severe penalties. The U.S. government has no jurisdiction and very little influence over the judicial systems in other countries.

An excellent resource on detailed health information entitled "Health Information for International Travel" is available for a fee from
Government Printing Office
Washington D.C. 20402
Phone: (202) 512-1800
or
Centers for Disease Control and Prevention
1-800-311-3435

Emotional and Mental Health

Emotionally and mentally, international living can be stressful. Most travelers will experience a degree of culture shock [see below] during the normal adjustment period. Culture shock causes feelings of disorientation and unease which can be intensified for students dealing with ongoing unresolved emotional or medical issues. It is thus very important that students with such problems discuss these with their study abroad advisors, mental health providers, or other trained medical personnel before leaving. Once on site, there may program staff available to help you through the adjustment cycle, but this is seldom guaranteed. Check with your program to see what psychological counseling is available, should you need it. Remember, study abroad is hard work and not therapy.

Nutrition

Be aware that you will probably experience a change in your diet and eating habits. You may start eating a healthier diet, as people in most countries don't eat as much processed food nor drink as many caffeinated and sweetened beverages as Americans do. It is customary in many countries to eat more grains, fresh fish, fruits, vegetables, etc. Before you leave, try to learn more about the foods eaten and the eating habits of your host country. These are an integral part of the culture.

Health Records

It's a good idea to bring a copy of your medical and dental records with you. If you have any ongoing medical or dental problems, bring a letter from your doctor or dentist explaining how they are being treated. Don't forget the telephone and fax numbers of your doctor and dentist, in case you need to contact them.

Medical Kit

Be prepared for minor health problems with a home medical kit. This should include:

- bandages, gauze, and adhesive tape
- sterile cleansers
- antibacterial cream
- painkillers
- anti-diarrhea medicine
- insect repellent (for any warm climate)

Medical and Accident Insurance

It is extremely important for you to have adequate insurance before departing. This coverage should also include medical evacuation, repatriation of remains and life insurance. If you are currently included on your family's insurance policy, you must make sure that the coverage meets your program's insurance requirements and is valid overseas for the duration of the program. Students with an International Student Identity Card (see International Student Identity Card) receive basic medical/accident insurance coverage for their travel outside the continental United States, for the period that the Card is valid. But such coverage may not be adequate to meet every contingency, so you should check to see what additional protection you might need.

Medical Care Abroad

Try to get some information about the health-care system in the region to which you're going. If you need medical care, what will the facilities be like? How do you pay for it? What legal right do you have to medical services? How are patients treated in your host country? (In some countries, doctors welcome questions from patients, while in others, patients are merely expected to follow doctors' orders.) You can get a list of English-speaking doctors worldwide by contacting:

International Association for Medical Assistance to Travelers (IAMAT)
417 Center Street
Lewiston, NY 14092

Family Emergencies

Discuss with your family what you will do in the event of a family emergency, illness or death. It is much easier to have these conversations around the kitchen table prior to departure than in an intercontinental phone call in the midst of a crisis.

Planning to be Safe

Remember there are no guarantees concerning personal safety anywhere in the world. Personal safety requires that you pay careful attention to your surroundings and act accordingly. The U.S. State Department issues several kinds of public announcements for travelers going abroad. Travel Warnings advise U.S. citizens of countries or parts of countries to avoid. Public Announcements warn about terrorist activity and other short-term threats. Consular Information Sheets have information for every country in the world about the crime risk and any areas of unrest, as well as issues such as visa requirements and the quality of medical care available. Contact the State Department at 202-647-4000, or visit their website at *travel.state.gov/travel_warnings.html*.

Get as much information as possible about the safety of your study abroad program before departure. Ask your program sponsor or a representative from your host school:

- What can you do to enhance your safety in the neighborhood in which you'll be living?
- If you're staying in a dormitory, what kind of security is provided?
- If you're living with a host family, have they been thoroughly investigated by the program? Have they hosted U.S. or other international students before?
- If there are program-related excursions, what kind of safety provisions have been made for them?
- Who is available on-site in case of an emergency?

For more safe travel tips, request the pamphlet "A Safe Trip Abroad" from:
U.S. Government Printing Office
Washington, DC 20420
202-512-1800

PRE-ARRANGEMENTS FOR RETURN TO HOME AND TO CAMPUS

Planning for departure also involves some planning for return to your home institution.

Pre-Registration

An important element to think about before you leave the country is which courses you will need to take on your return. Many colleges and universities allow their study abroad students to pre-register for the courses they will take upon their return. Students usually complete the paperwork prior to leaving and are then actually registered for their class either by the study abroad office staff or by the students' academic advisor. Make sure that you understand the procedure at your school so that you will get registered in the appropriate manner.

Housing

Depending on whether you plan to live in on-campus housing or off campus in an apartment when you return, you need to make your housing arrangements before you go. Some study abroad offices will send on-campus housing forms to you overseas to be completed or this may be done prior to departure. Check to see what the procedure is. If you are going to live in an apartment, you may even need to sign a lease and pay a deposit. You may even need to find someone to sublet your apartment during the time you will be overseas.

Transfer of Credit

If you are participating in a program that is not sponsored by your institution, there may be additional forms to complete. You may be required to take a leave of absence or you may need to actually withdraw from your school for the time period of your overseas study. Submitting readmission papers may be required. Will you get home institution credit or transfer credit for your course work? Your transition back into campus life at your school will be much easier if all paperwork is completed and procedures followed before your departure.

Learning About Your Host Country and Educational System

The Internet has become a valuable resource for learning about all aspects of other countries. Talk with faculty and study abroad returnees who have lived in your host country as well as international students from there. Get a personal perspective from them. Visit libraries and bookstores and contact the embassy, consulate or tourist office to get materials. Don't forget student-intended travel guides such as Let's Go and Lonely Planet Guide series. Read the international news section of your local newspaper or in internationally-oriented papers like the

New York Times, the Washington Post and the Christian Science Monitor. Watch newscasts and public television shows that talk about how the people live.

Another important aspect to learn about is the educational system you will be part of when you are overseas, especially if you will be studying at a foreign university. How do the faculty teach? How do the host country students learn? Will you be expected to be in class every day? What will be expected of you academically? Knowing the answers to these questions early on will allow you to set your own academic goals.

Preparing to be 'the American' Abroad

As you deepen your learning about your new culture, you should also be aware that in a foreign environment you will occasionally be put in the position of being a spokesperson about the United States and American culture. News accounts of happenings in the U.S. or foreign policy that moves around the world will cause some of your foreign friends and contacts to ask you searching questions. Are you sure you know enough about your own country? Returned study abroad students often remark on how they sometimes had a difficult time explaining the history, politics, and culture of the United States when pressed by their friends, much less in an academic classroom. They say they wish they had done some boning up on American history and looked at their own cultural values more critically before they went abroad. What are the American values? Will you be able to describe the characteristics of the American people to someone overseas — our social structures, our political system? Be prepared with some answers!

Top Twenty Subjects Searched on StudyAbroad.com
Indicative of most popular subjects studied while abroad

1. Business Administration	11. Theater
2. Art/Fine Arts	12. History
3. Computer Science	13. International Relations
4. Engineering	14. International Studies
5. Art History	15. Music
6. Psychology	16. Marketing
7. Education	17. Fashion Design
8. Biology	18. Accounting
9. Communications	19. Political Science
10. Economics	20. Design

PART IV: LIVING ABROAD

Knowing what you might expect when you first arrive in your host country can ease your transition to living abroad and help you make the most of the experience from the start. While what follows provides information and advice on how to avoid potential problems that could occur overseas, it is not meant to suggest that the experience before you — living and learning on foreign soil, in a culture not you own — is something you should fear. Indeed, it should be one of the most enriching, fulfilling, interesting, and educational experiences of your entire life.

This is what it has been, in any case, for nearly all students who have undertaken it.

ARRIVAL AND ORIENTATION

Immigration and Customs

When your plane lands in your host country, immigration officials will ask you the purpose of your visit and how long you propose to stay in their country. They will examine your passport, as well as visa and immunization certificates if they are required. They may or may not then stamp your passport, and you are free to enter the country. Depending on local practice, as well sometimes as the season and time of your arrival, this procedure can range from being quick and cursory to laborious and time-consuming. Even though you will be eager to exit the airport and start your study abroad adventure, it is important to be patient and respond very politely to any questions.

After Immigration, comes Customs. You will be asked to declare (perhaps in writing) if you are carrying certain items in your luggage. Be sure to declare any restricted items, as luggage may be opened and checked. Always be respectful and polite. Never make jokes about bombs or illegal drugs. This kind of behavior can get you detained by the police.

Student travelers are sometimes viewed suspiciously by Immigration and Customs officials. It helps to dress neatly and be well-groomed.

Jet Lag

In the first few days after your arrival, you are likely to experience physical changes as a result of taking a long flight and traveling through a number of time zones. You will probably be sleeping and waking at the 'wrong' times, feel tired, and have less patience than usual. This will pass within a few days, once your internal clock has adjusted to the time change. Another tip: upon arrival, get some exercise and do your best to wait to go to sleep until it is bedtime in the new time zone. This disorientation can be minimized some by avoiding alcohol and caffeinated products prior to and during your flight, and drinking plenty of other fluids. You may also want to set your watch to the time zone to which you are flying as soon as you get on the plane. Still, for most persons, some degree of short-term jet lag is inevitable.

On-Site Orientation

Many study abroad programs arrange for a representative to meet arriving students at the airport and transport them to the program site. Others will give directions, but ask you to find your way. If you are directly enrolling into a foreign university, there may or may not be someone to greet you and provide campus and local orientation. If your program does not offer on-site orientation, or if you will be directly enrolled in a foreign school, you will need to orient yourself to your new environment. Use the topics listed below as an overview of what you need to know:

The purpose of on-site orientation is two-fold: To review what you learned from your pre-departure preparations and to provide you with current site-specific information and perspectives about your surroundings which may not be possible at a distance and beforehand.

It is likely to cover the following areas:

Introduction to the program - Your registration for course work will be confirmed. You'll learn about the program rules and academic requirements, and you will be given information on social and cultural events and opportunities.

Health information - You'll be told about any special health precautions to take in the local environment.

Safety information - How to lessen the chance of becoming the victim of a crime or an accident while you are abroad and how to behave so as to maximize your personal safety vis-a-vis crime and violence.

Personal conduct - How to behave in ways appropriate to your status as a guest in your new environment. You cannot use the excuse of being "foreign" if you disobey the civil and criminal laws of the country.

Notifying local authorities - Your program representative should help you register with the local authorities, if this is required, and with the U.S. embassy or consulate so that you can be located in case of an emergency.

Housing - You may be taken to your dorm or apartment or introduced to your host family.

Language Training - Some programs offer basic training in the host language as part of orientation. Introduction to the local culture: lectures, tours, meetings, etc. on the local culture.

Communications - You'll be told about the options for keeping in touch with your family and friends at home.

Independent travel - Your program representative may be able to provide information on methods of travel, how to arrange it, and any safety factors involved.

Training - Most of what you need to be aware of will be provided, but the settling-in process must be lived through on an individual basis.

COURSE WORK AND CREDIT

As discussed in the first sections of this handbook, getting your planned course work approved by an academic or study abroad advisor before you go abroad is the best way to ensure that you get full academic credit for it. But this is not always possible, and even when classes are pre-approved, things may not work out as planned.

Q: What if one or more of your pre-approved classes isn't available, or you change your mind?
A: Contact your advisor at your home university immediately to ask for approval of substitution courses.

Q: What if you didn't know in advance what courses were available?
A: As soon as you know which courses you can enroll in, let your advisor know and request approval of the courses you've selected.

Q: What if you attend a U.S. college that approves study abroad courses only after students return?

A: Be sure to bring back information about all courses you took, including syllabi, reading lists, class notes, papers, tests, and portfolios. (This is a good idea for anyone who studies abroad, in case questions arise about how to evaluate a class or determine a grade.)

CULTURAL ADJUSTMENT AND EXPLORATION

Living and learning overseas successfully usually means adjustment to a different lifestyle, food, climate, and time zone, often accompanied by the necessity of learning to communicate in a foreign language. This process is never easy and can include mood swings alternating between heady exhilaration and mild depression. In the early weeks, you will probably feel excited about your new experiences and environment. Soon, you may find the excitement of new surroundings and sensations increasingly replaced by frustration with how different things are from home.

Culture Shock

This frustration and confusion is usually called 'culture shock.' Variations of culture shock can affect even experienced travelers and is considered a natural (and perhaps even essential) part of adjusting to a foreign culture. Symptoms can include depression, sleeping difficulties, homesickness, trouble concentrating, an urge to isolate yourself, and irritation with your host culture.

Even if you are used to being away from your family, you may still have problems. After all, you are now away from everything that's familiar. There are numerous ways to combat your feelings of disorientation until they pass (as they usually do):

- Learn as much as possible from local residents about their culture.

- Keep in touch with other American students. If you are directly enrolled in a foreign university, find out if there is a local hangout for American students. It can sometimes be helpful to meet with them and share experiences. Avoid letting these become gripe sessions, however.

- Keep yourself busy doing things you enjoy. When you have free time, visit museums, go to movies, and tour local sites of interest.

- Keep in touch with your family and friends at home. Letters, phone calls, or e-mail contact will make you feel less isolated.

- Try to keep your long-range goals in mind. Experiencing a new culture will inevitably involve some frustration and feelings of loneliness as you leave the familiar and incorporate the new, but they don't last forever.

- Don't overdo any of the preceding suggestions or you risk never making the adjustments to your new environment which are requisite to your purposes for being overseas.

In sum, since there is almost no way to avoid culture shock completely, you should try to accept it as something everyone goes through. Keep in mind that students returning from study abroad often describe working their way through culture shock as a necessary maturing experience, something that provided insight into their own cultural assumptions. You can ease your transition by recognizing the factors that cause culture shock and taking steps to minimize them.

For most students, the symptoms of culture shock wane after the first few weeks or months, as they begin to understand their host culture better. However, if you find that feelings of irritability and depression linger, you may need help from a doctor or counselor. Your program director or the international students office at your host university should be able to direct you to counseling or support organizations.

Fitting In and Being Accepted

Your study abroad experience will be heightened if you try as much as possible to become part of the local social environment. In the beginning, it is perhaps wise to behave like a guest, as indeed you are. For a while you may even be accorded a special status, that of a well-meaning (but not-quite-with-it!) outsider. But as time goes on, you will want to be able to behave in ways similar to that of the local students and citizens— and others will begin to expect such behavior of you. This means learning what behavior is and isn't appropriate in this new setting, and acting accordingly. Observe local students in your dormitory, on campus, on the street. If you live with a host family, see how family members dress and interact with one other and others. It's fine to ask questions about local customs and ways of behaving. In fact, people will appreciate that you are trying to learn about their culture and lifestyle, and are likely to help you adjust.

In some countries more than others, there is an unflattering stereotype of an American tourist, one who throws money around, drinks too much, is loud and rude, expects all foreigners to speak English, thinks the United States is better than any other country, and is always in a hurry. There are other countries in which all Americans are seen as happy, cheerful, carefree, and above all rich. Locals in your host country may assume parts or all of this to be true about you, simply because you are from the United States. Remember that their images of what 'Americans' are like are based on the other Americans they have seen, if not in person, then indirectly through our movies and media. Such is the nature of stereotyping. The challenge is to go beyond misleading images and false impressions, so that you and they can be yourselves, and mutual understanding can deepen over time.

Learning and Respecting Local Customs

'When in Rome, Do as the Romans Do' is not legal counsel, but rather seasoned advice to newcomers. Certain ways of acting in a country not your own affront local custom and show ignorance or disrespect, or both to local citizens. In many countries, for example, women traditionally cover certain parts of the body, such as the head, arms, and legs. In others, it is frowned on for couples to hold hands or display other types of physical affection in public. Most countries have customs associated with religion and sacred places. In certain Islamic societies, non-Muslims may not enter sacred sites. In Thailand, Buddhist monks must carry out an elaborate purification ritual if a woman touches them, including sitting next to them on a bus!

Understanding local customs will help you feel a part of the new culture and avoid potentially embarrassing situations. Especially if you are not fluent in the local language, your body language is often what expresses you. Saying hello or goodbye via a simple hand gesture is, for example, done quite differently from place to place, even within Europe. When to shake hands or kiss is signaled between people in different ways from country to country. How close to sit or stand when talking also varies greatly. These are just a few of the many simple habits for you to learn and then follow in order not to give unintended offense.

Brigham Young University's Culture Grams offer many insights on customs and lifestyles of individual countries. Phone 1-800-528-6279, or visit the BYU website at *www.culturegrams.com.*

Women Abroad

Appropriate behavior for young women varies from country to country, and even within countries. Some countries have well-defined gender roles. Others restrict certain activities for women, such as driving and meeting with men who are not relatives. You may find that behavior and dress that are acceptable in major cities are inappropriate in rural areas. Sometimes, though, just the opposite is true, and behavior is more relaxed outside of metropolitan areas.

Observe how local women your age act and dress and try to do likewise. In spite of your efforts, however, you may find that you are harassed. In some countries, women are routinely whistled at, pinched, and even grabbed — especially foreign women. This may be because, in some countries, the cultural stereotype of western women is that they are promiscuous. You can minimize unwanted attention by taking the following steps:

Dress modestly. Avoid sleeveless tops and short skirts, even in hot climates. Try to dress in the same style as the local women. Avoid making eye contact with men in the street. What may seem to you like simple friendliness might be interpreted as flirtation to a man from a country where women keep their eyes down. Watch the local women; see how they avoid and turn away unwanted attention, and mimic their behavior. Take a friend with you when you go out at night or to an unfamiliar area. In some countries, young unmarried women never go out alone. Arrange a public meeting place when you get together with people you don't know well.

Sexual Orientation

It is advisable to do some reading before departure regarding culture-specific norms of friendship and dating for relationships between people of any sexual orientation in the country where you are headed. Knowing about the culture-specific norms of friendship and dating for relationships between people of any sexual orientation in the country where you are headed is especially essential. Laws regarding same-sex relationships differ from country to country so you should inform yourself about those before your program begins.

Issues regarding sexual orientation are often included in materials prepared by study abroad offices and program providers. Check to see what information is available regarding GLBT issues from the programs in which you are interested. Travel guides, web resources, and your institutional GLBT office can provide additional valuable information.

For a bibliography regarding sexual orientation issues in countries outside the U.S, check the following Web site maintained by NAFSA: Association of International Educator's LesBiGay Special Interest Group: *http://www.indiana.edu/~overseas/lesbigay.*

STAYING HEALTHY

You have the best odds of staying healthy abroad if you come prepared, are careful about what you eat and drink, and don't engage in risky behavior that can jeopardize your health.

Food

The food in your host country is almost guaranteed to be different from what you're used to. In many places, the local diet may be based on meat, entirely vegetarian, very spicy, or just "odd" by U.S. standards — for example, the main staple may be rice or manioc root. While your stomach is still adjusting, you may wish to include some familiar foods in your diet. Look around for a western-style supermarket, and purchase some of the foods that you would eat at home. You are likely to find restaurants that serve familiar foods in major cities and tourist areas. You can probably also find U.S. fast food chains, for those times when you feel you need to have a burger or pizza. The point is that gradual adjustment and adaptation to the local diet makes social and usually nutritional sense.

The old adage for eating abroad is "Peel it, boil it, cook it, or forget it." Ask your program director, your host family, or local students if you need to take these precautions in your host country. If you do, peel all fruits and vegetables before eating them; anything that can't be peeled should be cooked thoroughly. This means no green salads. In areas where sanitation is poor, avoid unpasteurized milk and cheese made from unpasteurized milk. In some areas, it is unhealthy to eat food sold from stalls on the street. In others, "street food" is fresh and high quality. Consult friends from your host country before you sample food sold from stalls.

Can You Drink the Water?

Find out before you go whether the local tap water is drinkable. (In most Western European countries, it is.) If it isn't, drink bottled water. As an alternative, you can boil tap water for ten minutes, then let it cool; it will then be safe for drinking, cooking, and brushing your teeth. In restaurants, order bottled water if tap water is unhealthy, and don't request ice — it is usually made from tap water. If you are going to be hiking in a remote area where bottled water may not be available, bring a high-quality water filter or iodine tablets to purify water.

Diarrhea:

No matter how careful you are about what you eat and drink, you can still contract diarrhea. Travelers commonly experience this temporarily debilitating illness after a few days in a new country. In most cases, it lasts no longer than about five days, and the only treatment required is to replace lost fluids by drinking bottled water, fruit juice, or carbonated drinks. If diarrhea persists or is severe, contact a doctor.

Exercise

Regular exercise will help fight the culture shock blues and speed you through your initial jet lag. Throughout your time abroad, you'll feel more energetic and less stressed if you jog, swim, play tennis, or even go for a walk three or four times a week.

Alcohol Consumption

If you drink, drink sparingly. The customs regarding drinking wine and beer may be different in your host country than in the United States. The minimum drinking age may be lower, and it may be customary to drink wine or beer with meals. The result for some students is a problem with alcohol.

Drug Use

Illegal, addictive drug use is of course never good for one's health. Aside from the legal consequences, drug use can contribute to feelings of isolation and frustration. Further, anti-narcotics laws are strictly enforced in many foreign countries, whether a student is caught with a small amount of a drug for personal use or with a large quantity for sale to others. Young people, including Americans, are often targeted by police, especially in countries where the U.S. has complained about local enforcement of drug laws. According to the U.S. State Department, one-third of U.S. citizens arrested abroad are charged with possessing or using drugs. Worldwide, an average prison sentence for narcotics possession is seven years. In some countries, the sentence for certain drug charges is death. Never transport or deliver a package for anyone. If the package turns out to contain drugs, you can be arrested even if you were ignorant of its contents. To be safe, stay away from illegal drugs or anyone who uses or sells them.

AIDS and Other Sexually Transmitted Diseases

In some countries, HIV, the virus that causes AIDS, is a widespread health problem. Take the same steps to avoid this disease as you would at home. Use a condom if you are sexually active. (It may be a good idea to bring condoms with you, because the quality of condoms in some countries is unreliable.) Never share needles or use a needle that has been used before. This applies not only to injecting drugs, but ear or body piercing, tattoos, and acupuncture.

Other sexually transmitted diseases, such as syphilis and herpes, are also present worldwide. Use the necessary precautions to avoid these diseases.

Get up-to-date travel health advisories from the U.S. Centers for Disease Control and Prevention, *www.cdc.gov/travel.*

Travel Health Online offers links to physicians, U.S. State Department publications, and other health information. Contact them at *www.tripprep.com.*

STAYING SAFE

Dangers exist at study abroad locations, just as they do on or near U.S. college campuses. Problems can occur if and when students fail to take the same precautions abroad as they would at home. The best way to maximize your safety while studying abroad is to be aware of conditions that affect safety in your host country and any countries you plan to travel to; then adjust your behavior so that you take normal safety measures.

If you are enrolled in a study abroad program, listen carefully to the director when you are told about safety conditions and concerns in your host country. You can also receive general information by following the international news in newspapers and on all-news television channels such as CNN, though this is often sensationalized and does not accord with local accounts. Safety information on all countries is available from knowledgeable sources on campus, including the study abroad office, and from the U.S. State Department.

The most important factor in your safety abroad is likely to be your behavior. It's wise to do the following:

- Be aware of your surroundings at all times. Don't wander through unfamiliar areas alone, and always remain alert.
- Don't go out alone at night. Even when you're with friends, stick to well-lit streets where there are a lot of people.
- Don't flash jewelry, expensive cameras, or electronic equipment.
- Use caution when walking or jogging. Remember that in some countries, drivers use the left side of the road. In certain areas, drivers may not expect anyone to be running along the road.
- When crossing streets, keep in mind that pedestrians may not be given the right of way.
- Be careful with alcohol. If you drink, make sure it is only with people you know and trust, and designate one person to remain sober. As in the United States, never drink and drive. (Drunk driving laws abroad are sometimes much more severe than those in the United States.)
- Don't attract attention to yourself with provocative or expensive clothing or boisterous conversation in public. Observe local students' behavior, and try to mimic it.
- Use only official taxis. Unless meters are used, agree on the fare before you get in.
- Before you travel from your program site, find out what methods of transportation are safest and whether any roads should be avoided.
- Read the local papers to find out where high crime areas are and whether civil unrest is brewing.

- Stay away from demonstrations or any kind of civil disturbances. Even innocent bystanders can be hurt or arrested.
- Protect your passport. Keep it with you, in a front pocket or your purse. Be careful when displaying it.
- In general, avoid being engulfed in a crowd. This is the preferred environment of pickpockets.
- Accidents can happen anywhere. If driving, know what local traffic laws are and follow them. Always use a seat-belt. Make sure you understand local road signs and signals.
- Remain alert when walking. Before crossing streets, remember to look both ways; in some countries, traffic will be coming from the opposite direction from what you would expect.

OBEYING THE LAW

Whether at your program site or elsewhere, when you visit another country, you are that country's guest and are expected to follow its laws. They may be very different from those of the United States, which is why it is so important to find out what they are. Then be sure to follow them carefully— even if you feel they are repressive, irrational, or antiquated. Don't make the mistake of assuming that other countries will excuse illegal acts simply because you are a foreigner or a student. Even "minor" infractions, such as exchanging money on the black market or making purchases for foreign friends in hard-currency shops that are off limits for natives, can lead to severe penalties. Breaking a law will, at a minimum, get you dismissed from your study abroad program and possibly deported from your host country.

Try to understand the cultural context of these laws and regulations. If you disagree with them, it's fine to discuss your feelings with other North American participants in your program. You may also want to write about objectionable conditions in your journal. However, be careful about discussing your feelings with your host family or local students, until you know their views and the cultural context better. They may well be embarrassed to hear their country criticized. They may risk trouble by talking about issues that may not be discussed openly in their society. If you object so strongly to local laws or customs that you don't think you can follow them, it may be advisable to choose a different country. Talk to your study abroad advisor in the early stages of your planning.

U.S. notions regarding freedom of speech and expression have no parallel in many countries. It is important to realize that civil rights protections and U.S. legal procedures don't apply in other countries. People who are arrested are typically held without bail until their trial. Prison conditions in many countries can be wretched, and the U.S. idea of "innocent until proven guilty" may not apply.

U.S. embassies and consulates are able to offer only limited assistance to U.S. visitors who break laws. If you are arrested, they can contact your family and provide you with a list of local attorneys. They can visit you in prison to see that you are being treated humanely. They cannot, however, provide free legal assistance or money for bail. Most importantly, they cannot get you out of jail.

MONEY MATTERS
Buying and Using the National Currency
To live in a foreign country, you will need to learn how to use a new currency. Start by learning the exchange rate between U.S. dollars and the local currency before you leave home. Then try

to think in the local currency. Prior to departure, you can find out what the latest exchange rate is in your host country and other countries you plan to visit by contacting www.xe.com/ucc or any of many currency exchange websites. Remember that there will be daily fluctuations.

U.S. dollars can be exchanged abroad for the local currency at banks and exchange bureaus. Exchange rates vary slightly or significantly, from place to place and over time. In Europe, you can get acceptable exchange rates at railroad stations, and in some Asian countries, hotels may offer the best rate. Shop around for the best rate in your area. Don't be tempted by people who offer to exchange money on the street, or "black market." This is illegal in most countries.

If the U.S. dollar is strong, you can save money by exchanging all your money at once. As you near the end of your time abroad, remember to exchange only as much money as you'll need. In some countries, hard currency restrictions limit the amount of foreign currency that can be changed back into U.S. dollars, particularly if the original exchange receipts have been misplaced.

Exchange enough money at the airport exchange bureau to get you through the first few days. The exchange rate may be less advantageous than at a bank, but the convenience is well worth it.

ATMs Abroad

Automated teller machines (ATMs) are available in an ever-growing number of locations throughout the world, especially throughout Western Europe, connecting U.S. ATMs with those abroad. If your bank is part of an international network (check on this in advance) you can use your ATM card to obtain cash in the local currency from your bank account in the United States. Generally, the exchange rate is favorable because it's the same one the banks get when exchanging money.

In order to use ATMs abroad, your PIN code must be no longer than four digits. Be sure to memorize the numbers as well as the letters — some ATMs abroad have number pads without letters. Ask your bank for a worldwide directory of its ATMs. If your ATM card is part of the Cirrus network, you can find the location of these ATMs abroad by calling 1-800-424-7787. You can also get information on whether your host country has ATMs on your network by contacting: *www.mastercard.com* or *www.visa.com*.

Traveler's Checks

Traveler's checks are the safest way to carry money abroad. If they are lost or stolen, they can be replaced. Make sure you record the check numbers, and keep this separate from the checks. You can purchase traveler's checks in U.S. dollars, which are accepted in many countries worldwide. Traveler's checks are also available in other major currencies, such as Eurodollars, German Marks and Japanese Yen. Most banks and many travel agencies sell traveler's checks; they generally cost about one percent of the total amount you buy.

Getting Money in an Emergency

If you run out of money or an emergency comes up while you're abroad, there are several options for getting money from home.

Wiring Money

Cash or traveler's checks can be wired to you through companies such as Western Union or an American Express office (located in major cities). This service is fast but expensive.

Postal Money Orders

A family member or friend can buy a money order from a U.S. post office and send it to you. You'll be paid the amount of the money order at your local post office. Postal money orders have the advantage of being inexpensive, but the disadvantage of being slow: they take as long to get to you as an airmail letter.

Credit Cards

Credit cards are good for emergencies or major travel expenses. They also offer good rates of exchange. Before you go, find out what privileges cardholders with your credit card have when abroad.

Personal Checks

Some study abroad programs have an arrangement with a local bank to cash their students' checks. If yours does not, you are unlikely to be able to cash checks abroad. The exception is if you establish a bank account abroad, which may be a good idea if your program is for an academic or calendar year. In addition, some credit cards offer check-cashing privileges. At American Express offices abroad, for example, you can cash a U.S. check for up to $1,000 if you are an American Express cardholder.

Lost or Stolen Money

Record the toll-free service numbers for your credit card company, bank, and the company that issued your traveler's checks. If you lose any of them, or they are stolen, you can immediately contact the issuing company for instructions on how to get them replaced. Choose a credit card company that has offices in your host country, so you can get a replacement locally if necessary.

To keep your money as safe as possible, take the following precautions: Exchange money only in banks or other authorized exchange bureaus. Never exchange it on the black market. Carry only as much money as you need for a day. Use the same precautions when using ATMs (automated teller machines) as you would at home. The safest units to use are those inside banks or other buildings. Don't leave your purse unattended, even for a moment. Tuck it firmly under your arm; if it has a long strap, wear it across your chest rather than let it dangle off your shoulder. In some areas, a waist pouch or money belt may be the safest way to carry money, especially if it is worn under your clothing.

OTHER TIPS

Keeping in Touch

Communicating with people at home during your stay abroad can help put your parents' minds at ease. Staying in touch will also give you give you an opportunity to fill in your friends about what you're experiencing, keeping you connected to familiar circumstances and giving you a chance to begin telling your story.

Independent Travel

Visiting other areas of your host country and surrounding countries can help you understand other cultures. It's also just plain fun. But remember that permission from your college and parents for you to live and learn overseas, and the financial backing for this sojourn, was based on the assumption that course work taken as part of your U.S. degree studies is your central purpose. Travel away from your program site should be reserved for occasional weekend getaways, longer trips during program breaks, or extensive travel after your program ends. Such travel doesn't have to be a budget-buster if you do some advance planning for getting where you want to go and finding lodging while there. Most returned students say that getting to know one region really well is much more worthwhile than the superficial tourism that results from trying to see too many places in too short a period of time. You are young, and you are likely to be back, so it is best to resist temptations to race all over, merely accumulating fleeting glimpses and souvenirs to show off when you get back home.

Before You Return Home

Before you pack your bags, there are a few steps you need to take to make sure your return to the United States and your home campus goes smoothly.

Staying in Touch with Your New Friends

Get the addresses, phone and fax numbers, and e-mail addresses of people you want to keep in touch with. Maintaining friendships made abroad will ease your transition to life in the United States. And if you plan to return to your host country for graduate study or to work, you will want to be able to contact the people you know there.

Requesting a Transcript

Before you depart, make sure your transcript will be sent to your home university registrar. If the school you attended doesn't issue transcripts, request an official report listing the courses you took, your record of attendance, and an evaluation of your work.

PART V: REENTRY

Just as living abroad required you to make a number of adjustments, so does coming home. After all, you're not the same person you were when you went abroad. After spending anywhere from a month to a year living in a different culture, you have absorbed new knowledge and attitudes that have changed you intellectually and personally. While you're trying to find your new niche at home, you may wonder how to build on your study abroad experience. Like many returning students, you may want to immediately start planning to go abroad again.

CLEARING CUSTOMS ON RETURN

When you come back to the United States, you must pass through U.S. Customs, where you will be asked to declare the value of items that you purchased abroad that you are bringing back with you. Certain items are illegal to bring into the United States, and some require that you pay an import tax or duty. Currently, you can bring in souvenirs and gifts worth up to $400 without paying any duty. For items costing between $400 and $1,400, the import duty is 10% of fair market value. Above that amount, duty varies depending on the item.

There are two pamphlets available with complete information on Customs and duties: *Passports and Customs,* available for a small cost from:
Consumer Information Center
P.O. Box 100
Pueblo, CO 81002

or *Know Before You Go,* available free from:
U.S. Customs Service
Box 7407
Washington, DC 20044
Telephone: 202-927-6724

REVERSE CULTURE SHOCK

As odd as it may sound, you should prepare yourself for a period of cultural adjustment — or reverse culture shock — when you come back to the United States. Returning travelers experience the same physical and emotional upheavals as in the early stages of life abroad. This includes jet lag, as your body adjusts to the change in time zones.

In fact, many returning students are surprised to find that adjusting to life "back home" is more difficult than the adjustment they made to life in a foreign country. Why is this? While students understand that study abroad is a life-changing experience, many of them are not immediately aware of how they changed or how their experience abroad has caused them to look at life in the United States through different lenses. You may also experience a sense of loss after leaving your new friends and the life that you led while abroad.

After return, you may feel out of sync with friends and family, who may express only a polite interest in the experiences that you found fascinating. You might experience boredom and a lack of direction. You may also return to find that problems that were on hold while you were abroad — personal issues or career questions — are still waiting for you.

Some returning students experience particular difficulty reintegrating into the structure and expectations of academic studies. For that reason, it is advisable to allow some time between returning home and starting classes, if this is feasible.

CAMPUS REENTRY

Many U.S. colleges and universities offer reentry workshops to help students integrate their study abroad experience with their continued life and studies. Such workshops also allow students to talk about their experiences with people they know will appreciate them: other student travelers. They will encourage you to start new friendships with other students who have recently returned from abroad, as well as keep in touch with friends you made abroad.

Evaluate Your Program

Your home school may require you to complete a written evaluation of your studies abroad program. This can be a valuable experience for you, as it provides an opportunity to consider the pros and cons of the program you selected and reflect on what it meant to you. It may be even more valuable for future participants. Your evaluation will be made available to students who are considering studying abroad, as well as faculty and administration. A copy will also be send to your study abroad program, so program sponsors can learn what works and what needs improvement from the point of view of as many participants as possible.

Build on Your Experience

Even after you have readjusted to life and studies at home, you may want to build on your study abroad experience. Here are some options: Become a peer counselor for students who are considering study abroad, and help them make good planning choices. Volunteer as a "past participant" at orientations your study abroad advisor may be organizing for the next group of outbound students. Polish the language you learned by taking advanced language classes or joining a language club. Become involved with an international student as a roommate or tutor. Join an international organization. Pursue other opportunities to study, work, or travel abroad.

Career Planning

Your study abroad experience may propel you to begin searching for an international career as soon as you return home. The following will help you in this: Consult publications on working abroad, and pay attention to immigration policies in the countries that interest you. While you are abroad, make a list of contact information for anyone you meet who works in an area you're interested in. Once home, write to them to let them know that you are interested in returning abroad to work after you graduate. Prepare a resume, with the help of your university career center. Be sure to include your study abroad experience, language skills, and cross-cultural adaptation skills. Attend job-hunters' workshops that are relevant to your career goals. Find out if agencies and companies with offices abroad recruit on your campus. Investigate jobs in the United States that have an international focus. Look into teaching English as a Second Language abroad. Find out if you need a graduate degree to get the job you want. If so, which colleges offer that degree?

RESOURCES FOR STUDYING AND WORKING ABROAD

By William Nolting, University of Michigan International Center,
www.umich.edu/~icenter/overseas
2002

** = Best bets to start with, essential resources
* = Excellent for further exploration

WORLDWIDE STUDY AND INTERNSHIPS ABROAD

* ***Abroad View magazine.*** Subscription $10 for 4 issues, tel. 802-442-4827 or *www.abroadviewmagazine.com.* Quarterly features first-hand reports by students and faculty on their experiences abroad.

** ***Academic Year Abroad / Short-Term Study Abroad.*** (Annual). Institute of International Education (IIE – see Key Publishers). 720 pp. (AYA) / 530 pp. (STSA), $46.95 each plus $6 shipping. These are the most comprehensive and authoritative directories of study abroad programs, listing over 2,700 programs offered during fall and spring semesters (AYA) and 2,200 offered summer or short-term (STSA). Indexes for internships, practical training, volunteering, and student teaching list over 1,000 (AYA) and 520 (STSA) programs. Also indexed for subjects, cost, and more. Available at university study abroad offices. Free online at *www.iiepassport.org.*

* ***Advisory List of International Educational Travel & Exchange Programs.*** Annual. $17.50. Council on Standards for International Educational Travel, 212 S. Henry St., Alexandria, VA 22314; 703-739-9050, fax 703-739-9035; *www.csiet.org.* Lists programs for high school students which adhere to CSIET's standards.

** ***Directory of International Internships: A World of Opportunities*** edited by Charles A. Gliozzo and Vernicka K. Tyson. 2002. 5th edition. 160 pp. $25 postpaid from Michigan State Univ., Career Services and Placement, Attn: Directory of International Internships, 113 Student Services Bldg., East Lansing, MI 48824; 517-353-5589 ext. 146, fax 517-353-7254; *www.isp.msu.edu/InternationalInternships.* A comprehensive directory of both academic and non-academic internships located abroad. Profiles more than 200 internship programs. Cross-indexes for both subject & location.

* ***Glimpse magazine.*** Online at *www.theglimpse.com.* Features first-hand reports by students on their experiences abroad. Associated with Brown University.

* ***NAFSA's Internet Resources for Education Abroad,*** *www.secussa.nafsa.org* (click on "Internet Resources"). Website of professional association for study abroad has links to the best websites for researching study abroad, scholarships, work abroad, and international careers. It also has lots of information about health and safety abroad, financial aid, study in less-traditional locations, diversity in education abroad, and more.

**** *Peterson's Study Abroad.*** Peterson's. Annual. 1,170 pp. $29.95 , plus shipping from Peterson's (see Key Publishers). Detailed information on over 1,800 semester and academic year study abroad programs worldwide for college students, of which nearly 560 offer internships, listed in a special index.

**** *Peterson's Summer Study Abroad.*** Peterson's. Annual. 760 pp. $29.95 plus shipping from Peterson's. Detailed information on over 1,600 summer and short-term (up to 6 weeks) study abroad programs worldwide, of which around 260 offer internships, listed in a special index.

*** *Study Abroad: A Parent's Guide*** by William A. Hoffa. 1998. 112 pp. $15 from NAFSA (see Key Publishers). The only guide to respond to parents' questions and concerns about safety, academic credit, financial aid, program evaluation, travel documents, insurance, banking, and other issues related to study abroad. Not a directory of programs.

**** *Transitions Abroad magazine.*** Available from Transitions Abroad (see Key Publishers). $28/6 issues. Published 6 times a year, this is the only U.S. magazine which gives extensive coverage to all varieties of education abroad, from studying to working, volunteering and traveling abroad. And don't miss the great Transitions Abroad web site, www.TransitionsAbroad.com.

*** *Univ. of Michigan International Center's Overseas Opportunities Office (website),*** Web: www.umich.edu/~icenter/overseas, by William Nolting. Comprehensive collection of articles along with hundreds of selected annotated websites and books for study, scholarships and financial aid, internships, volunteering, teaching, and working abroad, plus international careers.

*** *The Unofficial Guide to Study Abroad*** by Ann M. Moore. 2000. 416 pp. $14.95. Arco/IDG Books. This book provides an in-depth introduction to all aspects of studying and working abroad. Not a directory of programs.

*** *A World of Options.*** Edited by Christa Bucks. 3rd ed., 1997. 658 pp. Mobility International USA. $35 individual, $45 organizations, members receive a 10 percent discount, from MIUSA, P.O. Box 10767, Eugene, OR 97440; 541-343-1284, fax 541-343-6812; info@miusa.org, www.miusa.org. A comprehensive guide to international exchange, study, and volunteer opportunities for people with disabilities.

FINANCIAL AID AND SCHOLARSHIPS FOR STUDY ABROAD

**** *Financial Aid for Study and Training Abroad 2001-2003*** edited by Gail Ann Schlachter and R. David Weber. 2001. 398 pp. $39.50 plus $5 shipping from Reference Service Press. Lists almost 1,000 funding sources available to support formal educational programs such as study abroad, training, internships, workshops, or seminars. Useful for high school, undergraduate and graduate students, postdocs; some listings for professionals. Indexes for level of study, location, and subject. This is the most up-to-date and comprehensive directory of scholarships for study abroad currently available.

*** *Financial Resources for International Study: A Guide for U.S. Nationals*** edited by Marie O'Sullivan and Sara Steen. 1996. 300 pp. $39.95 plus $6 shipping from IIE (see Key Publishers). Comprehensive directory of almost 700 funding sources based on a survey of over 5,000 organizations and universities in the U.S. and abroad. Lists funding sources available to support undergraduate, graduate, postdoctorate, and professional learning abroad, from study and research to internships, training and teaching. Indexes for level of study, subject, and organization.

**** *Institute of International Education*** (see Key Publishers), Web: www.iie.org. The IIE administers a number of study abroad scholarship programs. See their website for applications for scholarships available to undergraduates, including Gilman, Freeman-Asia, and NSEP. IIE also administers the Fulbright scholarships for graduating seniors and graduates.

*** *Rotary Foundation Ambassadorial Scholarships.*** Information available free from The Rotary Foundation of Rotary International, 1 Rotary Center, 1560 Sherman Ave., Evanston IL 60201-3698; tel: 847.866.3000; fax: 847.328.8554; web: www.rotary.org. This is one of the largest scholarships for study abroad available to undergraduates, graduating seniors and graduate students. Note that application is possible only through the Rotary Club in one's hometown or college town. Relatives of Rotary Club members are *not* eligible. Deadlines, set locally, range from March through July in the year prior to the study abroad year.

*** *Student Guide to Federal Financial Aid,*** U.S. Department of Education, annual. Available free from: U.S. Department of Education, PO Box 44, Washington DC 20044, or on the web at: www.ed. gov/prog_info/SFA/StudentGuide. Financial aid is the main source of funding for most study abroad students who have financial need. Be sure to consult with your own university's financial aid and study abroad offices!

WORK AND VOLUNTEERING ABROAD

*** *Alternatives to the Peace Corps: A Directory of Third World and U.S. Volunteer Opportunities*** by Joan Powell. 2001. 128 pp. $9.95 plus s/h from Food First Books; foodfirst@foodfirst.org, www.foodfirst.org. Order online or from LPC Group, 1436 Randolph St., Chicago, IL 60607; 800-243-0138. Thoroughly researched guide to voluntary service, study, and alternative travel overseas and in the U.S. with organizations which "address the political and economic causes of poverty."

**** *How to Live Your Dream of Volunteering Abroad*** by Joseph Collins, Stefano DeZerega, and Zahara Heckscher. 2002. 467 pp. $17. Penguin-Putnam. Web: www.volunteeroverseas.org. This highly-recommended book provides a comprehensive overview of volunteering abroad, including evaluations of over 100 volunteer abroad programs. Twelve chapters cover topics such as: Is Volunteering Overseas Right for You, Pros and Cons of the Peace Corps, Doing it Without a Program, Overcoming Financial Obstacles, How to Be an Effective International Volunteer, and Staying Involved When You Get Back.

**** *International Volunteer Programs Association (IVPA).*** Professional association for international volunteer programs sets standards for programs and lists those adhering to them on its website in a searchable database at www.volunteerinternational.org.

**** *Work Abroad: the Complete Guide to Finding a Job Overseas.*** Edited by Clay Hubbs, with Susan Griffith and William Nolting. 2002. 192 pp. $15.95 plus $4 s/h from Transitions Abroad. Comprehensive book from an American perspective with informative articles and hundreds of contacts and websites essential for success in the international workplace. Includes chapters on international careers, internships, volunteering and short-term jobs abroad, and teaching abroad. Order at www.WorkingTraveler.com.

**** *Work Your Way Around The World*** by Susan Griffith. 2001 (10th edition). 531 pp. Vacation Work (U.K.). $17.95 from Peterson's. The only guide to looking for short-term jobs while abroad. Extensive country-by-country narratives include first-hand reports.

INTERNATIONAL CAREERS

* ***Best Resumes and CVs For International Jobs: Your Passport to the Global Job Market*** by Ron Krannich and Wendy S. Enelow. 2002. $24.95 from Impact Publications. Definitive new guide includes over 100 examples of professionally produced international resumes and CVs for a variety of occupations and experience levels.

** ***Careers in International Affairs*** edited by Maria Pinto Carland and Michael Trucano. 2002. 7th ed. 282 pp. $17.95 from Georgetown Univ. Press, 800-246-9606, fax 410-516-6998. A comprehensive overview of international career fields. Survey of major organizations in all international sectors with insightful first-hand essays by practitioners. Developed by the Georgetown Univ. School of Foreign Service, this book is highly recommended for those serious about entering an international career.

* ***The Complete Guide to International Jobs and Careers*** by Ronald L. Krannich and Caryl R. Krannich. 1993. 349 pp. $24.95 from Impact Publications. A good introduction to strategies and skills for landing an international job. Should be used with its more up-to-date companion volume, *The International Jobs Directory*.

* ***The Directory of Websites for International Jobs*** by Ron and Caryl Krannich. 2002 147 pp. $19.95 from Impact Publications, www.impactpublications.com. Identifies more than 1,400 web sites for launching a global job search. The authors, renowned for their extensive career publications, also cover strategies for organizing an effective online job search.

* ***International Job Finder: Where the Jobs are Worldwide*** by Daniel Lauber with Kraig Rice. 2002. 345 pp. $19.95 plus $5.50 s/h from Planning/Communications, 7215 Oak Ave., River Forest, IL 60305; orders toll-free 888-366-5200; dl@jobfindersonline.com, jobfindersonline.com. Provides the latest information on over 1200 resources – web and print - for an international job search, including: specialty and trade periodicals, job hotlines, Internet job and resume databases, job placement services, avoiding job scams, directories, and salary surveys.

** ***The International Jobs Directory: A Guide to Over 1001 Employers*** by Ronald Krannich and Caryl Krannich. 1999. 334 pp. $19.95 from Impact Publications. A comprehensive source of hard-to-find information, tips on other resources including hundreds of web sites, and trends in international employment for Americans. Highly recommended. Should be used with its companion volume on strategies, *The Complete Guide to International Jobs and Careers*.

** ***International Jobs: Where They Are and How to Get Them*** by Eric Kocher with Nina Segal. 1999. 400 pp. Harper Collins. $17. Latest edition of a classic overview of international career fields and how to prepare for them, by authors associated with Columbia Univ.'s School of International and Public Affairs (SIPA).

* ***Jobs For People Who Love to Travel*** by Ronald and Caryl Krannich. 1999. 285 pp. $15.95 from Impact Publications. Information for those who want to work the world before settling down, including but going far beyond the travel industry. Explores motivations; 50 myths about jobs involving travel; includes internet sites, teaching abroad, and internships.

* ***Work Worldwide: International Career Strategies for the Adventurous Job Seeker*** by Nancy Mueller. 2000. 231 pp. $14.95. Avalon Travel Publishing. An in-depth look at strategies for finding international jobs. Covers topics such as researching, networking, resumes and job applications, interviewing, working abroad, and readjustment upon returning home.

TRAVEL ABROAD RESOURCES

* ***Centers for Disease Control and Prevention (CDC),*** tel: (toll-free) 888.232.3228 or 888.232.3299, website: www.cdc.gov/travel. This federal agency provides information on health conditions and recommendations for immunizations and tips on staying healthy in countries worldwide. Information available on their website or use their toll-free telephone service to hear announcements or order faxed information about specific countries or regions.

** ***Council Travel,*** tel: 800.2COUNCIL (to find nearest office), website: *www.counciltravel.com.*

This travel agency specializes in low-cost student tickets, railpasses and other items for student travel. Council Travel is owned by STA Travel.

* ***Currency Converter—Oanda,*** *www.oanda.com/convert/classic.* The Oanda converter allows for factoring-in different rates typical of credit-card and cash exchanges.

* ***Electronic Embassy,*** *www.embassy.org,* website only, connects to the websites of the U.S.-based embassies of foreign countries, which provide valuable information about visa requirements and cultural and travel information.

* ***Hostelling International—American Youth Hostels,*** HI-AYH National Office, 733 15th Street, N.W., Suite 840, Washington DC 20005; tel: 202.783.6161; fax: 202.783.6171; website: *www.hiayh.org.*

Hostels are the cheapest and friendliest accommodations worldwide. AYH is the American branch of this nonprofit international organization. You can get a Hostelling International membership card from them which is valid at hostels around the world.

* ***International Association for Medical Assistance for Travelers,*** 417 Center Street, Lewiston, NY 14092; tel: 716.754.4883; website: *www.sentex.net/~iamat.* Provides information on English-speaking doctors abroad.

** ***ISIC International Student ID Cards.*** STA Travel (see below) issues the U.S. version of the International Student Identity Card (ISIC). It is good for discounts abroad, can be used as a phone card with voicemail, and comes with an emergency assistance hotline and a small health and life insurance policy.

** ***Let's Go*** travel guidebooks, available in most bookstores or from St. Martin's Press, tel: 800.288.2131, website: *www.letsgo.com.* Travel guidebook series for low-cost student travel, authored by Harvard students.

** ***Lonely Planet*** travel guidebooks, available in most bookstores or from Lonely Planet Publications, tel: 800.275.8555, website: *www.lonelyplanet.com.* Travel guidebook series for low-cost travel to every world region.

* ***Mobility International USA (MIUSA),*** P.O. Box 10767, Eugene OR 97440, tel: 541.343.1284 (voice/TDD); fax: 541.343.6812; E-mail: info@miusa.org; website: *www.miusa.org.* MIUSA provides publications and videos on including persons with disabilities in international exchange and travel programs.

* ***Rail Europe,*** *www.raileurope.com.* Web site of a major US provider of Eurail passes has information about point-to-point tickets and rail schedules, in addition to information about Eurail and regional or country railpasses.

* *Rough Guide travel* guidebooks, available from most bookstores or from Rough Guides, 800.788.6262, website: *www.roughguides.com.* Travel guidebook series for low-cost travel.

** *STA Travel,* tel: 800.781.4040 (to find nearest office); website: *www.statravel.com.* This travel agency specializes in low-cost student tickets, railpasses and other items for student travel, and issues the U.S. version of the ISIC international student ID card.

** *US Department of State, www.state.gov* Essential help from the US government, for everything from travel safety advisories to crisis assistance for US citizens abroad, as well as contact information for all US embassies and consulates abroad. Also lists foreign embassies and consulates in the US. Frequently-consulted parts of this very comprehensive web site include the following.

•*Travel Warnings and Information, http://travel.state.gov/travel_warnings.html*

•*Travel Tips for Students, http://travel.state.gov/studentinfo.html*

•*Online US Embassies, Consulates, and other Missions, http://usembassy.state.gov/*

•*Services for US citizens abroad, http://travel.state.gov/acs.html*

•*Important Telephone Numbers* (for crises involving US citizens abroad, call 202-647-5225), *http://travel.state.gov/phone_faq.html*

•*Passport services (How to apply for a U.S. Passport), http://travel.state.gov/passport_services.html*

•*Foreign Entry Requirements* (for US citizens traveling abroad as tourists), *http://travel.state.gov/foreignentryreqs.html*

•*Foreign Consular Offices in the US* (where to apply for visas for other countries), *www.state.gov/s/cpr/rls/fco/*

•*A Safe Trip Abroad, http://travel.state.gov/asafetripabroad.html*

•*Travel Warning on Drugs Abroad, http://travel.state.gov/drug_warning.html*

•*Travel publications, http://travel.state.gov/travel_pubs.html*

•*Background Notes* (country information), *www.state.gov/r/pa/bgn/*

KEY PUBLISHERS

Impact Publications, 9104-N Manassas Dr., Manassas Park, VA 20111-5211; 800-361-1055, 703-361-7300, fax 703-335-9486; *info@impactpublications.com, www.impactpublications.com.* The best one-stop source for international career books published by Impact and many other publishers.

Institute of International Education (IIE), IIE Books, P.O. Box 371, Annapolis Junction, MD 20701-0371; 800-445-0443, fax 301-206-9789; *iiebooks@pmds.com, www.iie.org,* and *www.iiepassport.org.* Publisher of authoritative directories which list programs for studying, internships, and volunteering abroad. Also publishes a directory of scholarships for studying abroad. IIE's publications are available both as books and (free) online. IIE administers several scholarship programs, including Gilman, Freeman-Asia, NSEP, and Fulbright.

Intercultural Press, P.O. Box 700, Yarmouth, ME 04096; 800-370-2665 or 207-846-5168, fax 207-846-5181; *books@interculturalpress.com, www.interculturalpress.com.* Numerous publications dealing with cross-cultural issues, moving abroad, dealing with culture shock, and other issues related to working and/or studying abroad.

NAFSA Publications, P.O. Box 1020, Sewickley, PA 15143; 800-836-4994; fax 412-741-1142; www.nafsa.org. Essential publications for advisers and administrators in international educational exchange. For membership information, contact NAFSA: Association of International Educators, 1307 New York Avenue, NW, 8th Fl., Washington, DC 20005-4701, 202-737-3699, fax 202-737-3657; inbox@nafsa.org.

Peterson's, 202 Carnegie Center, P.O. Box 2123, Princeton, NJ 08543-2123; 800-338-3282, outside U.S. 609-243-9111, fax 609-243-9150; www.petersons.com. Publisher of guides to internships and careers, study abroad, and a U.S. distributor for many of the publications by Vacation Work (U.K.).

Reference Service Press, 5000 Windplay Dr., Suite 4, El Dorado Hills, CA 95762; 916-939-9620, fax 916-939-9626; webagent@ rspfunding.com, www.rspfunding.com. Publisher of numerous directories for scholarships and financial aid.

Transitions Abroad, P.O. Box 1300, Amherst, MA 01004-1300; 800-293-0373, 413-256-3414, fax 413-256-0373; info@TransitionsAbroad.com, www.TransitionsAbroad.com. Publishes Transitions Abroad ($28/6 issues), the only U.S. magazine that covers work abroad, education abroad, alternative and responsible travel, and living abroad. Also publishes books, *The Alternative Travel Directory* and *Work Abroad*.

ATTRIBUTIONS

These education abroad professionals have reviewed and contributed to the Student Guide, as a project of NAFSA's Section on U.S. Students Abroad, SECUSSA (see *www.secussa.nafsa.org*):

William Hoffa, Amherst College, Primary Author and Editor.

James Buschman, Syracuse University (Part I: Reasons for Studying Abroad)

Donna Mancini, Haverford College (Part II: Selecting the Program for You - Introduction through Location)

William Nolting, University of Michigan (Part II: How to Research Study and Internship, Volunteer and Work Abroad Opportunities; also Resources sections).

Charles Gliozzo, Michigan State University (Part II: Costs and Financial Aid)

Margery Ganz, Spelman College and Kathleen Sideli, Indiana University (Part II: Diversity)

Sally Raymont, Bowling Green State University (Part III: Before You Leave Home)

Heidi Soneson, University of Minnesota (Part IV: Living Abroad)

Pat Martin, University of Pennsylvania (Part V: Reentry) and project coordinator for SECUSSA.

STUDYABROAD.COM HANDBOOK ORDERING INFORMATION

Order Information:

Copies of the StudyAbroad.com Handbook can easily be ordered online using our Secure Order system.

- Please order copies of the StudyAbroad.com Handbook online: *http://www.studyabroad.com/handbook/orders.html*

- Call the StudyAbroad.com office (877/4040-EDU) to place your order.

Cost Information:

Single Copies: $7.95 (US) each

100+ Copies: $2.00 (US) each

Shipping Information:

Shipping is included for orders to the US & Canada.
Shipping for orders **outside the US & Canada is $2.00 (US) per copy**

The ONE CARD you'll need for Emergency & Worldwide Assistance

Medical, Personal, Travel &
Travel Safety Assistance
24 Hours a Day.
Online Services
and Pre-trip Information.

www.internationalsos.com

1-800-767-1403